BOSTON Herald

Boston Red Sox

2007 WORLD SERIES CHAMPIONS

SportsPublishingLLC.com

President and Publisher: Patrick J. Purcell
Editor-In-Chief: Kevin R. Convey
Executive Sports Editor: Hank Hryniewicz
Deputy Sports Editor: Mark Murphy
Director of Photography: Jim Mahoney
Chief Librarian: Al Thibeault
Vice President/Promotion: Gwen Gage

PUBLISHERS: Peter L. Bannon and Joseph J. Bannon Sr.
SENIOR MANAGING EDITOR: Susan M. Moyer
COORDINATING EDITOR: Noah Adams Amstadter
ART DIRECTOR: Dustin Hubbart
BOOK LAYOUT: Dustin Hubbart, Kayte Holleman, Doug Hoepker, and Laura Podeschi
IMAGING: Dustin Hubbart, Nic Mulvaney, and K. Jeffrey Higgerson

Front cover photo by Matthew West/Boston Herald
Back cover photos by Matt Stone and Matthew West/Boston Herald

ISBN: 978-1-59670-214-1 (softcover edition)
978-1-59670-213-4 (hardcover edition)

Printed in the United States

Sports Publishing L.L.C.
804 North Neil Street
Champaign, IL 61820

Phone: 1-877-424-2665
Fax: 217-363-2073
Web site: www.SportsPublishingLLC.com

Contents

Spring Training 6

Manny Ramirez 8

David Ortiz 10

Regular Season

April 5 at Kansas City 14

Terry Francona 16

Jonathan Papelbon 18

April 10 vs. Seattle 20

April 22 vs. New York Yankees 22

Mike Lowell 24

May 13 vs. Baltimore 26

May 29 vs. Cleveland 28

Kevin Youkilis .30

August 14 vs. Tampa Bay 32

Curt Schilling .34

August 21 at Tampa Bay 36

September 1 vs. Baltimore 38

Dustin Pedroia 40

September 15 vs. New York Yankees 42

September 28 vs. Minnesota 44

American League Division Series

Game 1 48

Game 2 52

Game 3 56

American League Championship Series

Game 1 62

Game 2 66

Game 3 70

Game 4 74

Game 5 78

Game 6 82

Game 7 86

World Series

Josh Beckett 92

Game 1 94

Game 2 100

Game 3 106

Game 4 112

World Series MVP Mike Lowell . .118

Celebration 120

Regular season statistics 128

BOSTON Herald

The entire staff of the *Boston Herald* photography department contributed to the coverage of the Boston Red Sox season, which culminated in a World Series victory. We gratefully acknowledge the efforts of staff photographers:

Michael Adaskaveg
Stuart Cahill
Ted Fitzgerald
Mark Garfinkel
Nancy Lane
Matt Stone
Matthew West
Patrick Whittemore
John Wilcox
Lisa Hornak
Angela Rowlings
and
Jim Mahoney, Director of Photography
Ted Ancher, Assistant Director
Arthur Pollock, Assistant Director

(Matthew West/Boston Herald)

Renewed optimism

By Jeff Horrigan
BOSTON HERALD
April 2, 2007

Only 2½ years have passed since one of the most glorious celebrations in Boston's storied history, but for many Red Sox fans, the final out of the 2004 World Series seems like eons ago.

Only eight players remain from the club that stunned the New York Yankees in the ALCS with baseball's greatest comeback before rolling over the St. Louis Cardinals in four straight World Series games. Busch Stadium, where first baseman Doug Mientkiewicz gloved closer Keith Foulke's throw to end 86 years of futility, was reduced to rubble and swept away. The Duckboats that carried the returning heroes through packed streets of Boston and along the lined banks of the river Charles now only tote tourists being told half-truths about the past, while unofficial mascot Nelson de la Rosa has passed on following a bizarre few months in the spotlight.

With the afterglow of the magical moment fading fast, it is no wonder that the organization has attempted to fire up the embers by rebuilding and reshaping the 2007 Sox. After landing Japan's top pitcher, Daisuke Matsuzaka, restructuring the bullpen and bolstering an uncharacteristically underperforming lineup with free agent additions J.D. Drew and Julio Lugo, the team departed Florida with the utmost expectations for this season.

"This certainly has to be one of the best Red Sox teams ever, if not best, going in," principal owner John Henry said in Fort Myers.

That optimism is a far cry from the end of last season, when the Sox finished below second place in the American League East standings for the first time since 1997 and failed to make the playoffs for the first time since 2002. Destroyed by injuries, ill-nesses and some apparent malaise, the club dispersed in early October with the hollow feeling of unfulfilled potential gnawing deep within its collective gut. Putting a personal touch on the old adage that whatever doesn't kill you will only make you stronger, Sox management vowed to do everything in its power to prevent a repeat performance in 2007. "It makes you determined to not let that happen again," Henry said. "You start your offseason earlier because it's something you want to avoid at all costs. The only positive aspect is we started early and laid out a game plan. Our No. 1 priority was Matsuzaka-san."

The landing of the former Seibu Lions star — which required a $103 million investment — has added an entirely new dimension to the Sox, who have suddenly became the focus of two nations. Matsuzaka gave every indication in spring training that he isn't going to disappoint, dazzling opposing hitters with his poise and wide array of virtually unhittable stuff. "He's worth every penny," Pittsburgh Pirates outfielder Chris Duffy said after facing Matsuzaka. "He throws every pitch imaginable and throws them all for strikes. With most pitchers, when you get in a hole against them, you at least have an idea what pitch they are going to throw to try to finish you off. With this guy, there is no sense sitting on a particular pitch because he throws everything."

The 26-year-old Matsuzaka should benefit from being nestled within a veteran starting rotation that could have three potential aces.

Curt Schilling turned 40 last November and appears determined not to let his age slow him down. The fact that the Sox informed him in

SPRING TRAINING

Manny Ramirez (left) felt right at home with Wily Mo Peña (center) and David Ortiz, walking in from the outfield together after Ramirez arrived in Fort Myers three days earlier than anticipated. *(Matthew West/Boston Herald)*

February that they have no intention of discussing a potential contract extension before season's end should only drive a highly driven man even more this season.

Josh Beckett, who will pitch between Schilling and Matsuzaka, has something to prove as well after being wildly inconsistent during his first season with the Sox. He posted a nifty 2.22 ERA in 16 wins but that number ballooned to 10.36 in 11 losses and 5.02 in six no-decisions.

The pitching staff received a boost in late-March, when the club returned Jonathan Papelbon to his former role as closer after initially making him a starter after last season as a precaution against further shoulder injuries. Papelbon, who diligently worked on strengthening the shoulder over the winter, was found to have one of the strongest ones on the team during physical exams in February and asked for the reassignment.

"This is something I would like to do for the rest of my career and kind of forget about starting and just go out there and chase records," Papelbon said. "Hopefully, what (Mariano) Rivera's done for the Yankees, I can do for the Sox."

Staying healthy will be a key. The team completely fell apart when catcher Jason Varitek was lost for the month of August to a knee injury. Varitek suffered through his worst offensive season in eight years — and the captain wasn't alone. Center fielder Coco Crisp fractured a finger during the opening week of the season and was never able to provide the type of offensive boost that the team expected after acquiring him from the Cleveland Indians. Mike Timlin, meanwhile, struggled for stretches after representing the U.S. in the inaugural World Baseball Classic, battling shoulder soreness throughout the season. Starting pitchers Tim Wakefield (rib cage) and Matt Clement (shoulder), outfielders Wily Mo Pena (wrist) and Trot Nixon (biceps), and shortstop Alex Gonzalez (oblique) also landed on the disabled list during a season that saw the team miss 793 man-games to injuries.

Slugger Manny Ramirez will also be a key. The left fielder, who in spring training vowed that he is happy here, started only seven games in the final seven weeks last season due to a knee injury, the severity of which some critics questioned. His absence left designated hitter David Ortiz without vital protection in the lineup.

The additions of right fielder Drew ($70 million, five years) and shortstop Lugo ($36 million, four years) should improve an offense that finished a disappointing 12th in the AL in team batting average and sixth in runs after leading the majors in each of those categories the three previous seasons. Both arrived, however, with their own question marks. Lugo's defensive abilities are not on a par with predecessor Gonzalaez, while Drew, who replaces Nixon in right, has been injury prone throughout his career.

Even so, optimism abounds.

"If we stay healthy, I'm pretty sure this is going to be a hell of a year," Ortiz said.

LEFT FIELD
MANNY RAMIREZ
ENJOY 'EM WHILE YOU STILL CAN

By Gerry Callahan
BOSTON HERALD
April 2, 2007

He'll be gone before George Bush and Dick Cheney leave office. He'll be gone before the oceans rise, the ice caps melt, and we all drown, which Al Gore penciled in for two years from Tuesday. He'll be gone before you know it, and even Manny Ramirez' harshest critics have to admit that Red Sox Nation will be a less colorful, less crazy, less interesting place.

Ramirez has two seasons remaining on his eight-year, $160 million contract, and then he'll be out of the Red Sox lineup and out of our lives for good. We're at T-minus 19 months to liftoff from Planet Manny, and then the man will disappear into Red Sox history, never to appear at NESN again.

Among his many other honors we can add this to Manny's resume: Least Likely to Return for Any and All Reunions of the 2004 World Series Championship.

Enjoy him for the next 324 games (minus a hamstring pull or two) because we'll never see him or another player quite like him again.

The Sox have two option years on Ramirez' contract, but if they even think about picking them up it will be the biggest upset since Seal hooked up with Heidi Klum. Consider this: Manny signed his contract six years ago — before Theo, before John Henry, before Hazel Mae and monster seats and gorilla suits and 38pitches.com. To this day he remains the second-highest paid player per year, trailing only Alex Rodriguez, who signed his 10-year, $252 million deal in the same gluttonous offseason.

Manny will be 36 at the end of the 2008 season. He told the *Herald*'s Karen Guregian this spring that he'll likely continue to play after his current contract expires, which is fine. He doesn't have to go home then, he just can't stay here.

There is no doubt that Boston will miss Manny, but make no mistake, not nearly as much as Manny will miss Boston. It is the enduring irony of the Manny era: He has made it clear many times he wants out of this baseball-crazy place, a place that happens to be perfect for him.

Boston offers, among other things, the easiest defensive position in baseball for the defensively challenged Ramirez, and a better lineup around him than Barry Bonds has had in his career. This year, the Sox invested $70 million in J.D. Drew, who, if healthy, will hit fifth and make certain that Manny will see more good pitches than he has in years.

At the top of the lineup, Julio Lugo, Kevin Youkilis, and David Ortiz will make it difficult for Manny to drive in 125 runs. The Sox, with their $160 million payroll, are certain to contend for a division title and a playoff spot, which should keep even Manny interested through most of the summer.

And if it doesn't, if Manny decides to milk a sore hammy for a month or more, what's the big deal? The fans will forgive him. His teammates will defend him. The ballclub will excuse him. Red Sox Nation will keep on loving him.

Manny might find a less baseball-obsessed place to play in 2009, but he'll never find a city that is more tolerant of his quirks or his craziness. The Red Sox expanded the clubhouse to keep him happy. They hired a guy who sits in the dugout in uniform but is neither a player nor a coach. Ino Guerrero is there primarily to keep Manny happy because a happy Manny produces like few players in baseball.

During the first week of spring training, the Sox held a players-only meeting to discuss how to best handle Ramirez' late arrival. They agreed that, at least for public consumption, they would insist it was no big deal. They stuck up for him even though he sat down on them at the end of last season. Add it all up, and it's a better deal than A-Rod's.

Like no team in sports, the Red Sox love to celebrate big events, and there is a big one coming later this season. Manny will hit his 500th home run (he has 470), essentially guaranteeing his election to the Hall of Fame on the first ballot, as if there was any doubt. For this one moment, the Sox probably wish Manny could be more like Bonds and intentionally tank it on the road so the home fans could enjoy the milestone. On the all-time home run list, Manny will pass, among others, Willie Stargell, Stan Musial, and Lou Gehrig. Strike up the band, Dr. Charles.

When Manny hits his third homer this season, probably sometime in the next week or two, it will mark an interesting milestone in his career. It will be No. 237 since he came here from Cleveland, meaning more than half his homers will have been hit in a Red Sox uniform. By the end of the year, more than half his RBI and games-played will have come here, too.

For those who keep track of such things, it will soon be set in stone. Manny Ramirez will represent the Red Sox in Cooperstown. And since they did not dominate until it was too late, Curt Schilling and David Ortiz probably don't have a realistic shot to join him.

Manny is the lone Hall of Famer on your '07 Sox.

We know he'll ask to be traded at some point, and we know the Red Sox won't trade him. They'll put up with him because he'll put up the numbers, and then 19 months from now, they'll say goodbye. And down the road, the Sox will put together an extravagant event to celebrate Manny Ramirez' incredible career. And they'll know, in their hearts, there will be zero chance of Manny showing up.

(Matt Stone/Boston Herald)

DAVID ORTIZ

BIG PAPI: FRONT AND CENTER

By Tony Massarotti
BOSTON HERALD
April 2, 2007

FORT MYERS — The simple truth is that his reputation now precedes him, even in places far, far away. How else to explain what David Ortiz has become, what he means to the Red Sox and to major league baseball?

"You've often heard me say that we're in the Golden Era of baseball. David Ortiz, Big Papi, symbolizes that Golden Era," baseball commissioner Bud Selig said over the winter. "He's been such a great player on a grand stage, but it's his personality along with his ability that has made him an important part of this sport.

"I have enormous respect for David Ortiz. He's conducted himself so beautifully off the field as well as on the field," Selig went on. "I'm very proud of David Ortiz, for a myriad of reasons. It's everything about him. . . . He stands as a great symbol for the success of this sport — and a symbol for all of the right reasons."

So here we are now, starting the 2007 baseball season with a Red Sox team that is rapidly developing a worldwide following. The Red Sox have players from Japan, Puerto Rico, the Dominican Republic and the United States on their Opening Day roster. Their following spans from Taunton to Osaka to Santo Domingo and San Juan, further proof that the Sox are now a global enterprise, a booming baseball Disney.

But no matter where Red Sox fans are, ask them to identify the team's greatest ambassador and the indisputable face of the franchise — the face, perhaps, of baseball — and they all come back with the same answer.

Papi.

"Similar to Big Papi, he has a very bright, open personality," Red Sox newcomer Daisuke Matsuzaka said during spring training when asked about Manny Ramirez.

You see?

Ortiz is used now as a baseline comparison, a measuring tool in all corners of the world.

Even Matsuzaka has learned that, and he just got here.

On the field, there is no disputing what Ortiz has become. Over the past four seasons, Ortiz leads all major leaguers in RBI (525) and ranks seconds in home runs to only fellow Dominican Albert Pujols (179-173). That is true despite the fact that Ortiz did not begin playing regularly until almost halfway through the 2003 season, his first as a member of the Red Sox.

In the beginning, after all, even the Red Sox did not understand what they had stumbled upon.

"People are scared of him," said Red Sox shortstop Julio Lugo, formerly a member of the Tampa Bay Rays, when asked how other teams regard the Ortiz who stands in the batter's box. "People are scared of making a mistake."

Of course, that has been truest when the stakes have been highest, a development that began during the 2003 season. After struggling for much of the Red Sox' first-round series against the Oakland A's, Ortiz delivered a game-winning hit against then-A's reliever Keith Foulke in Game 4 at Fenway Park. The hit helped send the Sox to the 2003 American League Championship Series and set the foundation for the 2004 playoffs.

What has happened since has defied logic and undermined conventional baseball wisdom. Beginning with the 2004 playoffs, Ortiz has 11 walkoff hits, seven of them home runs. Nine of his 15 career walkoff hits are homers, including three last season, when he ended five games with a mighty swing of his bat.

Along the way, Ortiz set the Red Sox' single-season home run record (54 last season) and became

the first Sox player ever to lead the All-Star Game in fan balloting. He did that in 2005, which served as the final aftershock on his amazing 2004 playoff run.

"Obviously, you had to be under a rock to not see what he did in the playoffs last year," Red Sox pitcher Matt Clement said at the 2005 All-Star Game. "It shows the kind of presence he's become in baseball."

Early last season, the Red Sox signed Ortiz to a four-year, $52 million contract that will keep the slugger in Boston through at least 2010. But following a winter during which salaries skyrocketed and lesser players scored big, Ortiz now seems like such a bargain (at an average salary of $13 million per season) that Red Sox officials surprised him with a brand new pickup truck at the start of spring training.

Could it be that Sox officials are feeling guilty?

"No," said a reluctant, almost embarrassed Ortiz.

He paused momentarily.

"Maybe," he said with a smile.

Still, if Red Sox officials are guilty of being disarmed by their slugger, they can be forgiven; Ortiz seems to have that effect on most everyone. Baseball is a business and business is cold, yet Sox officials similarly bestowed Ortiz with an unneces-

sary gift in 2005, when owner John Henry presented Ortiz a plaque that declared him "the best clutch hitter" in Red Sox history.

Opponents, too, frequently find themselves eager to meet Ortiz, encounters that usually happen when players from both teams are stretching and doing wind sprints just before a game. According to Ortiz, he is sometimes greeted by players he does not even know — they almost always call him "Papi" — which speaks to his approachability, one of his greatest assets.

Last season, even former Sox ace and current New York Mets right-hander Pedro Martinez acknowledged that Ortiz, along with Pujols, has surpassed Martinez in popularity in their native Dominican Republic.

"He could be the president of the Dominican Republic right now, that's how popular he is," said Lugo, also a Dominican native. "He's very caring and he's done a lot of good things. He goes out in public and he's not afraid to say hi to you, and it doesn't matter how rich or poor you are. He's very humble and people like that."

President Papi.

Has a ring to it, eh?

REGULAR SEASON

Nothing lost in translation

IN DEBUT, DICE-K AS GOOD AS ADVERTISED

By Jeff Horrigan
BOSTON HERALD
April 6, 2007

KANSAS CITY, Mo. — As the Red Sox' designated hitter, David Ortiz enjoyed being able to retreat to the visitors clubhouse during an unseasonably chilly afternoon yesterday.

But while his purpose was to study video of his at-bats — he struck out four times in five plate appearances — Ortiz couldn't help but focus on the live feed from the field, where new teammate Daisuke Matsuzaka turned in an incredible effort in his major league debut.

"Every pitch he throws, when you watch on TV, is like a Nintendo game, man," Ortiz said after the 4-1 victory over the Kansas City Royals. "He throws pitches that just disappear at the plate."

With millions in Japan stirring at 3 a.m. to observe the historic moment, it was only appropriate that Matsuzaka was lights-out. The 26-year-old right-hander allowed only one run on six hits, struck out 10, and held the Royals hitless in three at-bats with runners in scoring position.

"It's a day I've been waiting for for a very long time," said Matsuzaka (1-0), who fell one strikeout shy of Don Aase's club record for K's in a major league debut (July 26, 1977). "Given that fact, it felt surprisingly normal."

There was little normal about his vast array of pitches, which mesmerized and overpowered Kansas City's batters.

"He reminded me of Pedro (Martinez) the way he pitches," Ortiz said. "He's in total control of the game when he's out there."

Terry Francona was just as impressed.

"The expectations so far, from what I hear, are unreachable, but he's got this figured out better than anybody else," said the manager, whose club took the final two games of the season-opening series. "He loves to pitch, he enjoys the heck out of the game, and he's pretty damn good. That's good enough for me." Opposing starter Zack Greinke took a tough loss. In his first start for the Royals since 2005 — social anxiety disorder forced him to spend most of last season in the minors — the 23-year-old right-hander allowed one earned run on eight hits and a costly walk. He struck out seven.

Greinke, who left trailing 2-1 after seven, fell behind right away in the first. He walked Kevin Youkilis with one out and then surrendered a two-out, run-scoring double off the right-field fence to Manny Ramirez.

The score remained 1-0 until the fifth, when Julio Lugo punched a leadoff double down the right-field line, stole third, and scored when catcher John Buck's throw sailed into left.

Matsuzaka, meanwhile, allowed a base hit to David DeJesus to open the first but didn't give up another until the fifth. He walked Mark Teahen with one out in the first but escaped unharmed by starting a double play off an Emil Brown comebacker.

Matsuzaka marooned a pair of runners in the fifth and then surrendered his only run in the sixth when DeJesus belted an 0-and-1 fastball over the right-field fence. Esteban German followed with a base hit, but the potential shift of momentum was halted one batter later when Matsuzaka struck out Teahen and catcher Jason Varitek threw out the runner attempting to steal second.

Daisuke Matsuzaka has words with catcher Jason Varitek in the fifth inning. The Japanese pitcher struck out 10 in his major-league debut.
(Matt Stone/Boston Herald)

Matsuzaka, who topped out at 104 pitches during spring training, threw 96 pitches through six innings but returned for the seventh and set down the side in order, striking out two batters before getting Buck to fly out.

The Sox gave him and his relief some breathing room in the eighth by scoring a pair off reliever Joel Peralta. Ortiz led off with an opposite-field double, took third on a Ramirez flyout, and scored on a wild pitch. Coco Crisp, who had been hitless in his first nine at-bats of the season, later knocked in the fourth run with an RBI single.

BOSTON 4, KANSAS CITY 1

TERRY FRANCONA

TITO MANAGES JUST FINE

By Steve Buckley
BOSTON HERALD
April 10, 2007

Life would be easier for Terry Francona if managing the Red Sox were no more complicated than filling out a lineup card and then waiting until the sixth or seventh inning for the obligatory pitching change.

But this is the 21st century. This is Boston. And this is why managing the Red Sox is one of the toughest jobs in professional sports: You're expected to be a modern-day, high-tech, laptop-toting, on-base-percentage-obsessed, outfield-shifting skipper who must do his work in a city whose fans know the name of the backup catcher at Single-A Greenville and whose sportswriters could find a controversy in a clubhouse checkers game.

"This city can be draining," Francona said one morning during spring training in Fort Myers. "But I do try to take care of myself. I go home and go to bed, or to go to bed. I don't have the energy that I used to, and this job takes it out of you anyway. So if it's going to give somewhere, it's not going to be at the ballpark. I need to have the proper amount of energy and enthusiasm at the ballpark. So if it has to give someplace else, it does."

Look at it another way: Francona, entering his fourth season as manager of the Red Sox, must deal with health issues on two levels.

One, there is the health of his players.

Two, and of most importance to his family, there is his own health.

In 2002, Francona suffered a pulmonary embolism. On April 6, 2005, Francona grew faint as the team bus was traveling to Yankee Stadium for a day game. Francona wound up being rushed to a New York hospital and spent several days under observation for what was termed a virus.

The manager also has battled crippling knee injuries, to the point that on many nights he has ice packs attached to his legs during his postgame press conferences.

This past offseason, Francona resolved to heed the advice he is always giving to his players: Take care of yourself. He vowed to smell the roses, so to speak, and to spend more time away from the ballpark. As a result, a fresher, more relaxed Francona arrived in Fort Myers in February.

"When the season's over you press the off button," he said. "That's just the way it is. You kind of operate on autopilot during the season, and then, when it's over, I kind of collapse."

As he prepared for this season, Francona also resolved to give up smokeless tobacco, which is as much a part of a big league clubhouse as pine tar.

"(David) Ortiz spit his out the other day when he came out of the game, and I almost dove on it," Francona said. "What he does is, when he's done hitting, he spits his out. And I wanted to hit the floor and finish it."

Francona said he underwent a complete physical before spring training, which, he pointed out, raised no red flags. As he put it, "So now, if I have a bad day, it's not like I feel like I'm having a heart attack. I'm just having a bad day."

There will be bad days. Again, this is Boston. Though there were no major brouhahas in spring training — no so-called Manny Moments, no serious injuries to star players, no shocking trades — there were still the occasional moments in which Francona refused to suffer fools gladly. Just last week, as he was grilled by reporters as to why Daisuke Matsuzaka decided not to hold a media session following his start against the Cincinnati Reds, Francona said, "You guys are going to drive me nuts."

To Francona, it's a Boston thing. He never felt the media/fan scrutiny during his playing days in such towns as Cleveland, Montreal, and Milwaukee.

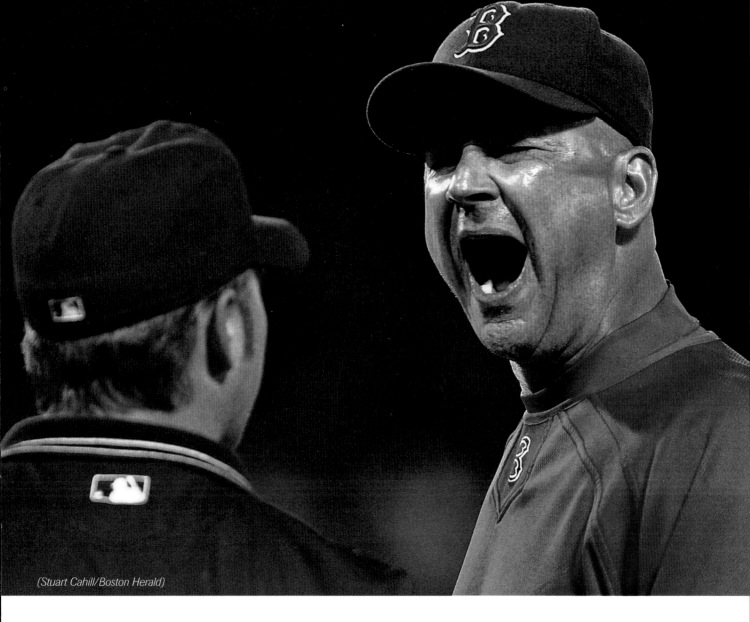
(Stuart Cahill/Boston Herald)

Surprisingly, he didn't feel it during his days managing the Philadelphia Phillies.

"When I was in Philly there was a lot of apathy," he said. "It's still an East Coast town, but the team was down. The level of interest when I came to Boston was at an all-time high. When I was at Philly it was probably at an all-time low. So there is a difference.

"When something goes wrong here, there are a lot of people who want to know why. And I don't BLAME that. I'm not MAD about it. But I'm the manager, and it's my responsibility for us to get through this, let's move on, and we'll fix the problem."

A year ago, Francona went into a weight room at Fenway Park and ran into old friend and then-Oakland A's manager Ken Macha. They exchanged pleasantries and gossip, as managers will do, during which Macha talked about the difficulties of managing the A's.

"I remember when he left, thinking to myself, 'He has no idea,'" Francona said. "He has no idea of what my day consists of. But at the same time, if I were in Pittsburgh or Kansas City, I don't think I'd feel any differently, either. Everybody's got their job to do. Sometimes I read the Tampa papers when I'm down here (in spring training), and it's almost like cheerleading. And I don't like that, either.

"I actually like what's going on with the media in Boston. There are some days when you get aggravated. I don't mind somebody saying, 'Why did you do this,' or, 'Why did you do that.' If I don't have an answer, then I'm not a very good manager. But just because a writer disagrees, that doesn't mean much anyway, because I know what the hell I want to do."

JONATHAN PAPELBON

THRILL OF THE KILL FUELS PAPELBON SHOW

By Gerry Callahan
BOSTON HERALD
April 10, 2007

He stares in for the sign like another No. 58, Jack Lambert, staring across the line of scrimmage and into the quarterback's frightened eyes. The play hasn't yet begun, but the play is almost over. The battle is almost won. He hasn't yet thrown a pitch, and already the batter is down in the count and drowning in self-doubt.

Dogs smell fear, and so do closers. They smell it and they stoke it, and then they go in for the kill. Sometimes they do things for effect, for intimidation purposes only. They stare at the ground in concentration and then turn deliberately, intensely, toward the target, glaring at their opponent like a boxer at center ring. They exhale purposefully, and you can almost see the flames.

If baseball is all about anticipation, then this is one of the great moments in every Red Sox fan's day: waiting for Jonathan Papelbon, anticipating his charge out of the bullpen, his routine on the mound, his ability to overpower the best hitters in the sport and allow the Sox to win a game they had no business winning.

Any more questions? In a way, the whole tedious closer debate went down as dramatically and as convincingly as poor Michael Young did on ESPN Sunday night. The guy has 200-plus hits for four straight seasons. He's a three-time All-Star, a batting champ, a genuine superstar. And Sunday night, eighth inning, runners on first and third and one out, he had no chance, none, zero.

It was like the reverse of that new A-Rod TV commercial where the young kid morphs into Alex Rodriguez as he digs into the batter's box. Young dug in, looked out at Papelbon, and instantly appeared to be about 4-foot-10 and 98 pounds. There are not many who could make Michael Young turn into Eddie Gaedel on national TV. The only thing that could have made the moment any better is if

some wise ESPN person had pulled the plug on Joe Morgan, who is still trying to figure out who's going to pitch the ninth.

Maybe this is the part we overlooked through the whole closer contest in January, February, and March. The Sox didn't just have a willing and able closer in young Papelbon. They had, potentially, a great one, a transcendent short reliever who could, if healthy, infuse the whole club, hell, the whole region with confidence and swagger and attitude. It's what Mariano Rivera did for the Yankees through four World Series championship seasons in the late '90s, and it's what Papelbon can do for the Sox as long as he stays healthy. It's much more than any No. 4 starter could ever do.

You can argue the value of 220 innings for a healthy starter vs. 70 for a closer, but ask yourself this: When was the last time a starter threw $1\frac{2}{3}$ innings that meant as much as the five outs Papelbon got in Texas Sunday night? Maybe it was only one game in early April, but it was one game they would have lost without Papelbon at the back end of the bullpen. And it would have been a demoralizing blow to everyone from starter Curt Schilling to slugger David Ortiz (two homers) to reliever Joel Pineiro, who made a mess of the eighth inning before handing the ball to Papelbon. Off the hook, everybody.

The only people happier than Red Sox fans to see Papelbon back in the closer's role are Red Sox players.

"Frickin' unbelievable," said Schilling, summing it up for everyone in the clubhouse.

Papelbon was supposed to be handled carefully this season after his shoulder gave out after 59 appearances last summer. But Sox manager Terry Francona called on him with one out in the eighth because Papelbon was the difference between win-

ning and losing, and he even managed to get Tito off the hook. Five outs in 15 pitches? Power pitchers aren't supposed to do that.

He has now been a closer for a calendar year, and aside from the injury, he has been off the charts. Last year his 0.92 ERA was the eighth-lowest in major league history (minimum 50 innings). Opponents hit .167 against him, tying Pedro Martinez, in 2000, for the best in club history. And how does he like hostile environments? In his career, he has thrown a total of 18 innings in New York, Toronto, Baltimore, and Texas. He hasn't allowed an earned run yet.

The Red Sox got lucky. Papelbon has all the ability to be a great closer, but it takes much more than that. It takes a certain mentality, a passion for the job that you don't often find in 26-year-old power pitchers. Usually they want to be Roger Clemens.

Papelbon wants to be a Mariano Rivera, God bless him. In the long run, he'll make less money. He'll play less golf. He'll sleep less, sweat more. He doesn't care. Jack Lambert didn't want to play quarterback, and Jonathan Papelbon doesn't want to start. That's a good thing for all of us.

If the Red Sox take a three-run lead against Seattle today, let's hope they stop there. Let's hope we get to see Papelbon in the ninth, staring, glaring, breathing fire. There are lots of reasons to make it to Fenway for the home opener. No. 58 is No. 1 on the list.

Score early, often in record-setting rout

BOSTON BATS EXPLODE AS BECKETT SINKS MARINERS

By Jeff Horrigan
BOSTON HERALD
April 11, 2007

Overcast, gusty and raw, with gloomy, grey clouds parting to provide only sporadic glimpses of the sun, the Back Bay assumed the uncomfortable feel of Warsaw throughout most of yesterday afternoon.

Brazen, unmasked bandits held up those wishing to park cars anywhere remotely close to Fenway Park for the price of a mortgage payment, while all-but-stagnant lines everywhere moved at the pace of the Registry of Motor Vehicles during lunch breaks.

As far as nearly 39,000 folks were concerned, however, it could not have been a more ideal day.

An afternoon that began with the honoring of the 1967 Impossible Dream team ended with the thorough reinforcement of the region's realistic vision for October, as the Red Sox delivered the most convincing victory in 96 Fenway home openers with a 14-3 pounding of the Seattle Mariners. The 11-run margin eclipsed a 15-5 thrashing of the New York Yankees in 1973.

"We pulled out the whuppin' stick today a little bit," said winning pitcher Josh Beckett, who won his second consecutive home opener.

The right-hander dominated the Mariners, allowing only one run on two hits in seven innings, while striking out eight and walking none.

Beckett (2-0) offered a complete contrast to Mariners starter Jeff Weaver, who seemed to have more rust than an old, tin roof after not having pitched since March 31 because of Seattle's four consecutive days of inclement-weather postponements in Cleveland. Weaver, who pitched the clinching game of the World Series for the St. Louis Cardinals back in October, was a complete mess and lasted only two innings, allowing seven runs on seven hits and two walks. The righty threw 70 pitches (only 37 for strikes).

"I think (the layoff) definitely took a toll on them as far as being able to pound the strike zone," Beckett said. "You can't go through our order and walk guys. You're going to get burned 100 percent of the time."

The Sox took full advantage of Weaver's spotty command and jumped out to an immediate 4-0 lead in the first inning before tacking on three more runs in the second, including a pair on J.D. Drew's two-run home run swatted into the center field bleachers. Drew (1-for-2, sacrifice fly, three RBI) has at least one hit in each of his first seven games with the Red Sox and an 11-game hit streak extending back to last season with the Los Angeles Dodgers.

"Your home fans are what you want to pay homage to and really have a good home opener and it worked out well," Drew said. "It couldn't have worked out any better. You get a chance to score a lot of runs and get a chance to hit a big home run in your first game here. It was special."

Drew and Beckett were far from the only ones to shine. New shortstop and leadoff hitter Julio Lugo reached base all four times (2-for-2, double, two walks, RBI, two runs). Catcher Jason Varitek, who came in hitting just .125, went 3-for-4 (double, walk, three RBI), while first baseman Kevin Youkilis finished 3-for-5 (two doubles, two runs, RBI).

"It's a nice way to play the game, when you score first and then add on," manager Terry

APRIL 10 VS. SEATTLE

Josh Beckett throws a pitch in the first inning against the Seattle Mariners during the Red Sox home opener at Fenway Park. The Red Sox ace collected his second win of the season in Boston's 14-3 victory. *(David Goldman/Boston Herald)*

Francona said. "That's a good recipe for winning."

The only imperfection on the field occurred in the eighth inning, when Sox reliever Brendan Donnelly was ejected for hitting Kenji Johjima with a pitch, one batter after he nearly scrapped with Jose Guillen following a strikeout of his former Angels teammate. Hideki Okajima came on following the ejection to finish the eighth and was followed in the ninth by Mike Timlin, who came off the disabled list before the game.

BOSTON 14, SEATTLE 3

Sox wield power broom

FIVE HRs CAP OFF SWEEP

By Jeff Horrigan
BOSTON HERALD
April 23, 2007

The late start for Daisuke Matsuzaka's official indoctrination into the Red Sox-Yankees rivalry occurred just as Monday morning rush hour was beginning in Japan, meaning that things might have been significantly quieter on Tokyo's roadways than usual.

But while the 9 a.m. start in the pitcher's homeland may have eased the morning commute, it was Matsuzaka's teammates who brought traffic to a halt around Fenway Park with a record-setting offensive performance in a 7-6 victory that completed the three-game series sweep.

Matsuzaka (2-2) was only so-so, but still managed to snap a personal, two-start losing streak, despite allowing six runs on eight hits in seven-plus innings and neglecting to hold a middle-innings lead for the second straight outing.

The Red Sox offense, however, provided room for error by clobbering five home runs, including a major league record-tying four straight in the third inning.

Manny Ramirez, J.D. Drew, Mike Lowell, and Jason Varitek hit consecutive homers off New York starter Chase Wright to erase a 3-0 deficit, but Matsuzaka surrendered individual runs in the fifth and sixth to allow the Yankees to regain the advantage, 5-4.

"There's no way I could be satisfied," Matsuzaka said through a translator. "What I wanted most of all was to hold the lead, and I couldn't do that. When I get the chance again to pitch in New York next week, I will be conscious of it and I will do my best not to repeat the problems I had."

Lowell wrested the lead back in the seventh inning by slamming a three-run shot over the Green Monster off reliever Scott Proctor.

Lowell's 12th career multi-homer game (and first since May 20, 2004), allowed the Sox to sweep their archrivals in a series of at least two games for the first time since April 23-25, 2004. It was the first such sweep at Fenway since August 31-September 2, 1990.

"They're a little bit broken down with injuries and, if anything, that's the time to take advantage, because they're going to make their run," Lowell said.

Wright, who was making his second big league start, walked a tightrope in the first two frames, but managed to strand two runners each time. The 24-year-old left-hander retired the first two batters in the third before suddenly losing all effectiveness, as well as his 3-0 lead.

Ramirez, who entered the game batting only .193, started things by smashing a 91 mph fastball beyond the Monster seats. J.D. Drew followed by jumping on a slider and blasting it over the Red Sox bullpen for his first home run since the home opener on April 10.

Lowell then demolished a changeup, slamming it over everything and onto Lansdowne Street. Jason Varitek completed the historic barrage by walloping a fastball over the Monster for his second homer of the series.

"I just wanted to hit the ball hard to keep the momentum going," Lowell said. "I got a hold of one and the dugout was going crazy. It was really cool, a

APRIL 22 VS. NEW YORK

Mike Lowell is congratulated by Julio Lugo after he hit a three-run home run in the seventh inning. It was Lowell's second home run of the game. *(Matthew West/Boston Herald)*

unique feeling."

The power surge marked the fifth time in major league history that a team hit four consecutive homers in an inning, and the first since the Los Angeles Dodgers did it vs. San Diego last September 18. No American League team had accomplished the feat since the Minnesota Twins vs. the Kansas City Athletics on May 2, 1964.

It was the 10th time in Sox history that they've hit four homers in a single inning and the first since July 23, 2002 vs. Tampa Bay.

BOSTON 7, NEW YORK 6

THIRD BASE
MIKE LOWELL
IN MARLINS, SOX REELED IN A WHOOPER

By Tony Massarotti
BOSTON HERALD
May 13, 2007

When the Red Sox made the trade, remember, their front office was in a tumultuous state. Theo Epstein had resigned and was actually in a cab, on his way out of the country, when the Sox formalized the deal that brought Josh Beckett and Mike Lowell to Boston.

So the Red Sox gave up the 2006 National League Rookie of the Year in Hanley Ramirez.

They just might have made the deal that has been the biggest key to their 2007 season so far.

"We gave up some things, but I think the Red Sox have benefited greatly from Beckett and Mike Lowell," said Bill Lajoie, the former Red Sox advisor who helped oversee the team's baseball operation during Epstein's absence in the fall and winter of 2005. "The thought was right. It just happened a year later than sooner.

"It was myself and Craig Shipley who were the proponents of that trade, who wanted to go for it," Lajoie said. "There were some last-second attempts to stop the trade, but we decided to go through with it."

Let's make something clear here: No matter how big a star Ramirez becomes, it will not matter to the Red Sox as long as Beckett continues to be what he is. That is indisputable truth. The cost for pitching being what it is, no price is too high for a 27-year-old who is blossoming into a legitimate staff ace.

And right now, before our very eyes, that is what is happening here.

Six or seven months ago, when Ramirez was named Rookie of the Year and Beckett was coming off a season in which he allowed 36 home runs, the question in Boston concerned blame. Now Beckett appears to be taking the next step in his development and Lowell is off to a terrific start after a solid 2006 campaign, and suddenly the question in Boston concerns praise.

Who, exactly, was responsible for this deal?

Now, as then, we hold certain truths to be self-evident. Despite Epstein's role as Deep Throat during his absence, there was strong indication in November 2005 that Epstein was against the Beckett deal. (You'll just have to trust us on this one.) The Red Sox were operating with a four-horsemen front office of Lajoie, Shipley, Jed Hoyer, and Ben Cherington, two older men and two younger ones, debating the benefits of a bird in hand vs. two in the bush.

Ultimately, it appears, Lajoie and Shipley won out. (Lajoie, too, went out of his way to credit Sox president Larry Lucchino for expressing faith in them during the unsettling time.) Lajoie and Shipley both are regarded as tremendous evaluators of talent — Shipley in particular, does not get enough credit for this skill — who were willing to take on Lowell and his contract (on which $18 million remained) because they believed he and Beckett would help the club.

They were right.

"There were two people in evaluation within that organization that I trusted (at the time), and that was me and Shipley," Lajoie said. "We had a lot of faith in (Lowell) because we'd seen him play well (for) too many years. When I was over there (scouting) and watching him play, he tried everything to get out of it (during a miserable '05 season). He tried to hit the ball to right field and it would get caught, or he'd line out to the second baseman. There was nothing wrong with the player. It was just that kind of a season."

Based on Lowell's play since, Lajoie and Shipley now look like seers. Last season, while playing Gold Glove-caliber defense at third base, Lowell finished with more home runs (20) and RBI (80) than any Red Sox players but David Ortiz and Manny

Ramirez. And while Lowell endured uncharacteristic defense struggles earlier this year, he entered yesterday batting .304 and on a pace to finish with 33 home runs and 133 RBI.

This season, in fact, Lowell has ranked second in OPS among American League third basemen to only the otherworldly Alex Rodriguez.

So, while Beckett was the centerpiece of the trade, the truth is that Lowell has given the Red Sox their money's worth, and then some. Lowell is 33 and eligible for free agency at the end of the season, but he has been productive enough since the start of last season that he cannot be viewed solely as simply an anchor in the deal that brought Beckett to Boston.

Along with Beckett, the Red Sox also landed a productive, veteran third baseman who has brought to the clubhouse both a dignified presence and leadership.

(Nancy Lane/Boston Herald)

"There's a premium for frontline pitching, so let's be realistic. I mean, Josh was the key to that deal," Lowell said. "But I like to think there was some belief that I'd be able to produce. (The Marlins) didn't trade me because I was old. They traded me because of the contract. I'm aware of how things work.

"It's an appealing situation (in Boston). I like the way the organization does things," added Lowell, who said that he has not had any discussion with the Sox regarding a contract extension. "We go for a World Series every year. We're not rebuilding, ever, here. I want to be in that flow I had in '03 (when he and Beckett were on a World Series-winning Marlins team). I don't want that to be the only time in my career."

As for Beckett, let the record show that Epstein, too, was smart enough to recognize a good thing. Though Beckett struggled for chunks of last season, Epstein signed Beckett to a three-year, $30 million contract extension that also includes a $12.5 million option for 2010. Even if the Sox pick up the option, they will end up with four years of Beckett's services for $42.5 million, an average of $10.6 million per season — far less than what the Texas Rangers are paying Vicente Padilla or the Kansas City Royals are paying Gil Meche.

And if Beckett continues to pour it on today against the Baltimore Orioles and beyond, that (and Hanley Ramirez) are a very small price to pay for a bona fide big league ace.

25

Sox' stunning comeback a holiday treat

SIX-RUN NINTH DELIVERS WIN OVER ORIOLES

By Jeff Horrigan
BOSTON HERALD
May 14, 2007

For 8½ innings yesterday, it appeared that the only Bostonians who were going to round the bases at Fenway Park were the moms invited to celebrate their special day with a postgame romp on baseball's hallowed ground.

After all, with the way Baltimore Orioles pitcher Jeremy Guthrie dominated the Red Sox for eight nearly flawless frames, there was no reason to believe that what transpired in the ninth would lead to the mother of all comebacks.

Trailing by five runs with one out in the bottom of the ninth, the Sox took full advantage of sloppy defense and a questionable pitching change by manager Sam Perlozzo to stun the Orioles, 6-5.

The Sox rallied for six runs against relievers Danys Baez and Chris Ray, winning on Julio Lugo's infield single and Ray's error, which erased a 5-4 deficit and sent the Sox to their largest last-minute comeback in almost a decade.

The last time they rallied from a ninth-inning deficit of five or more runs and came back to win was April 10, 1998, when they erased a 7-2 deficit against the Seattle Mariners and won the home opener, 9-7, on Mo Vaughn's walkoff grand slam off Paul Spoljaric.

"(It is) a combination of some magic here and some really good players that don't quit," Sox manager Terry Francona said.

The win, coupled with the New York Yankees' loss in Seattle, gave the Sox an eight-game lead in the American League East standings, their largest cushion since Sept. 30, 1995 (also eight games).

The only negative aspect of the day was pitcher Josh Beckett having to come out after only four innings due to what the medical staff termed an avulsion, or small cut on his right middle finger. It is too early to tell if Beckett will make his next start on Friday.

Beckett endured multiple blister problems with the finger during his days with the Florida Marlins, but he insisted that yesterday's issue was different.

"It is not a blister," Beckett said. "My skin just tore. There is nothing there. It's not like I got a blister under my callus. It's just one of those deals where you have to wait and see."

Yesterday's victory was the Sox' first walkoff win this year. "This team never thinks the game is over until it's over," Lugo said. "We never give up. That's the character of this team."

For eight innings, the only character that anyone was talking about was the right-hander Guthrie, who totally neutralized the Sox, allowing only three hits and not permitting a runner to advance past second base.

Guthrie opened the ninth by retiring his eighth consecutive batter when Lugo grounded out, and he then induced a soft pop from Coco Crisp in front of the plate. However, catcher Ramon Hernandez dropped the ball for an error, which was compounded by Perlozzo's different kind of error. He brought on Baez, who gave up an RBI double to Ortiz, followed by a single to Wily Mo Pena.

"That was kind of weird," Ortiz said of the pitching change.

Ray then came on and walked J.D. Drew and Kevin Youkilis to force in a run before Jason Varitek

MAY 13 VS. BALTIMORE

David Ortiz watches his ninth-inning double, which scored Coco Crisp for the Red Sox' first run. Boston scored five more in the inning for a 6-5 come-from-behind victory. *(Tim Correira/Boston Herald)*

doubled to drive in two runs, making it 5-4. Baltimore intentionally walked Eric Hinske before Youkilis was forced out at the plate by Brian Roberts on Alex Cora's chopper.

Lugo then ran the count full before bouncing a ball to the right side of the infield. First baseman Kevin Millar fielded the ball and threw to Ray cover-ing at first, but the pitcher, perhaps distracted by the sliding Lugo, missed the ball, allowing Varitek and Hinske to score and sending Fenway into bedlam. The play was scored as an infield single, with an error to Ray.

"That feels pretty good," Ortiz said. "At one point, it looked like we had no shot."

BOSTON 6, BALTIMORE 5

Beckett picks it right up

RIGHTY RETURNS STRONG

By Michael Silverman
BOSTON HERALD
May 30, 2007

The word of the day at Fenway Park yesterday was "beat."

As in, Josh Beckett (8-0) did not miss a beat being out two weeks because of a cut in his right middle finger.

Also, the Red Sox beat the Cleveland Indians, 4-2, setting themselves up for a sweep tonight against the second-best team in the American League.

And, the beat goes on for the Sox, who can do little wrong with their balanced attack and fundamentally sound style of play. Their record is the best in the majors at 36-15, and their lead in the AL East is 11½, 14½ on the last-place Yankees.

Beat that.

"This is a really special group of guys and we pull together," said Beckett, who allowed just one hit and no runs in his first six innings before giving up a pair of runs on two hits in the seventh. "We're pulling on the same end of the rope. We don't have a lot of the he-said, she-said stuff going on that I know I've been a part of in other clubhouses. This is just a real special group of guys."

Tops among the special cast of characters who supported Beckett on his first outing since May 13 was Kevin Youkilis, who is swinging a scalding bat. With his second home run in as many nights and his 13th double of the month, Youkilis extended his hitting streak to 21 games (.441) and had his ninth multi-hit game in a row.

"I've seen a lot of good players but he's a really good, young, improving hitter that is feeling good about himself, that's for sure," Sox manager Terry Francona said.

Youkilis knocked in the first run in the first inning with the double off Jeremy Sowers (1-5), and Jason Varitek doubled the lead with a leadoff homer (No. 5) in the fifth. Youkilis led off the two-run sixth with his solo home run (8). The Sox worked three walks in a row in that inning off reliever Fernando Cabrera for a second run, but the long inning probably did not help Beckett with his results in the seventh inning.

A single, triple and groundout produced two runs but the important thing for Beckett was that after 91 pitches, his blister-prone finger was not an issue at all.

"If you can take anything good out of that seventh inning it's that my finger didn't blow up on me," said Beckett. "The bullpen came in and did a great job. We scored enough runs. It was a good win."

Beckett went on the disabled list after the cut appeared in his May 13 start. The fact that the Sox were oblivious to the absence of their best starter by going 11-4 speaks volumes about the special roll they are on right now.

"I think we were smart with this thing," said Beckett. "The medical staff, trainers, everybody was real supportive. They even got some hand specialists and surgeons in there and those guys definitely didn't go unnoticed in this thing. (Medical director) Dr. (Tom) Gill and those guys, they stopped at nothing to make sure that we nipped this thing in the bud."

Although the tips on the fingers of Beckett's right hand will have to be monitored for the remainder of his career, a return outing like last night's can do wonders for the confidence of the still-young pitcher.

And his team as well, not that confidence is any problem right now.

MAY 29 VS. CLEVELAND

Josh Beckett throws to first base keeping Jhonny Peralta on base in the first inning of Boston's 4-2 victory over Cleveland. Beckett collected his eighth win. *(Matthew West/Boston Herald)*

BOSTON 4, CLEVELAND 2

KEVIN YOUKILIS

DEFENSE NEVER RESTS FOR EMERGING SOX STAR

By Jeff Horrigan
BOSTON HERALD
May 25, 2007

ARLINGTON, Texas — With a .347 batting average, a .429 on-base percentage and a 16-game hitting streak, Kevin Youkilis' ability to get on base for the Red Sox is no longer in question.

And as the 28-year-old's breakout season progresses, his ability to keep opponents *OFF* base with stellar defensive play at first is becoming more evident each game.

In only his second full season at the position, Youkilis has quietly fortified a reputation as one of the most adept-fielding first basemen in the American League. In 39 starts there this season, the former full-time third baseman has handled all 355 chances without an error, extending his errorless streak to 94 games dating back to July 4, 2006.

"I didn't have a chance to see him play third base that much, but it looks to me like he's been playing first base all his life," infielder Alex Cora said. "He works hard at it, which is the most important thing, but when you watch him, you realize he's a natural from the get-go."

A third baseman throughout his amateur career at Sycamore (Ohio) High School and the University of Cincinnati, Youkilis' only extended experience at first before the majors occurred in 2002 at Single-A Sarasota. There, he was moved across the diamond for a few weeks to accommodate then-favored third-base prospect Tony Blanco.

Youkilis took over as the Sox' starting first baseman in spring training 2006, after the team's offseason efforts to acquire several veterans failed. He understandably looked uncomfortable at times early in the transition phase but still managed a .995 fielding percentage (five errors in 1,035 chances), which ranked fourth among regular AL first basemen.

Naturally, everything seemed different when the second year rolled around. His footwork became second nature. He better understood the limits of his defensive range. And he handled short-hop throws without the slightest bit of anxiety.

"I think the biggest thing is just having a year under my belt playing first base," Youkilis said. "Last year was more hands-on experience and getting used to it. Nothing catches you too off-guard anymore. You know where you're supposed to be, what you're supposed to do. Now it's just more natural. You're not questioning yourself all the time. First base is now just first base."

Cora, who's played all four infield positions, said he particularly appreciates Youkilis when he's playing one spot over at second.

"Looking at the big picture, just having someone with so much range there really helps the team," he said. "When I'm playing second base, I know I have another regular infielder next to me and I know I can give a little more to my left, knowing he plays so much off the line. That helps you so much, knowing you don't have to worry about your left side (because) you can move to your right. It helps not only getting to balls but with double plays because you get to (second base) earlier to turn it."

As time goes on, Youkilis' deftness handling off-the-mark throws has stood out. He may yet to be in the class of Gold Glovers like J.T. Snow and Doug Mientkiewicz but clearly has their potential.

"He works so hard on his picks and taking groundballs," second baseman Dustin Pedroia said. "He's a good athlete, which is huge for a first baseman. It's great because if you dive up the middle or something, you try to miss down (with the throw to first base), and you know we're going to have a chance because he's so good at picking

(Matthew West/Boston Herald)

balls. Naturally, I'm trying to hit him in the chest (with the throw), but obviously, that's not going to happen every time. He's got real good hands, which is one of the biggest things when you're picking balls out of the dirt."

Meanwhile, Youkilis' ability to keep the ball away from opposing fielders currently is drawing the most rave reviews.

He enters tonight's series opener at Texas as one of baseball's hottest hitters. He's batting .443 (31-for-70) during a career-best 16-game hitting streak (only Derek Jeter's 18-game streak currently is longer) that's included four home runs, 13 runs scored and 16 RBI. Along the way, he's had 12 multiple-hit games, giving him an AL-best 20 this season. He's had at least one extra-base hit in his last five games.

"We're seeing a guy mature right in front of our eyes," manager Terry Francona said.

Youkilis, however, hardly is impressed.

"I just love playing every day," he said. "In 2005, when I got sent up and down so many times (between the Red Sox and Triple-A Pawtucket), I think I came to realize how great it is to be up here and how exciting it is just to be in the lineup. Hopefully, I've got a long career ahead of me, and this is just the start."

Rally caps work for Sox

LESTER'S EFFORT NOT FOR NAUGHT

By Jeff Horrigan
BOSTON HERALD
August 15, 2007

On a night when Jon Lester made a Fenway Park comeback that many Red Sox followers feared they would never see, it was only fitting that his teammates also made a remarkable comeback.

Lester pitched seven fantastic innings but was on the verge of absorbing a difficult-to-swallow defeat to the Tampa Bay Devil Rays before the Sox rallied for their eighth final at-bat victory, the second in walkoff fashion.

Mike Lowell tied the score by clobbering a tape-measure home run onto Lansdowne Street off Tampa Bay reliever Al Reyes with one out in the ninth inning before Coco Crisp sent the Sox to a 2-1 victory by following Jason Varitek's two-out, ground-rule double to right field with a game-winning single to right on a full-count changeup.

"It's nice to see our guys jumping on each other," manager Terry Francona said. "We haven't seen that a lot."

The Sox had been 1-41 when trailing after eight innings. Their only other walkoff win occurred on Mother's Day, when they erased a 5-0 deficit against the Baltimore Orioles with a six-run rally in the ninth.

The victory pushed the AL East lead over the Yankees, who were thumped by the Orioles, 12-0, in New York, back to five games.

Lester, who hadn't appeared in a Fenway game in nearly a year, was outstanding, save for a brief lapse in the fourth inning. He fully rebounded from a rough, 3 ⅓-inning outing in his previous start to allow just a pair of hits, while striking out four and walking only one. Both of the hits occurred in suc-cession in the fourth inning, a Carl Crawford double and B.J. Upton single setting up a Carlos Pena sacrifice fly.

"I'm glad (Lester's) efforts didn't go to waste," Lowell said. "That would've been a shame. This is a nice story — not something you see every day, especially in sports — but he's a good pitcher and we're going to need him."

It appeared the fourth-inning run would be enough support for Tampa Bay lefty Scott Kazmir, who held the Sox to four hits in six dominant innings, while striking out eight. Relievers Gary Glover and Dan Wheeler followed with scoreless innings before Reyes squandered only his second save chance in 19 opportunities.

Kazmir, who has allowed only one run in his last 25 innings, lowered his ERA since the All-Star break to 1.01 ERA.

"He's a phenomenal young lefty," Francona said. "He had all of his pitches working tonight and he pretty much had his way with us offensively."

Lester, who made his first four starts on the road following his July 23 recall from Triple-A Pawtucket, last pitched at Fenway Park on August 18, 2006, when he was involved in a minor fender-bender on Storrow Drive on his way to face the Yankees. Shortly after the outing, Lester developed back pain that resulted in a string of medical examinations that uncovered his affliction with anaplastic large cell lymphoma. He made one more start, on August 23, before landing on the disabled list to begin what ultimately proved to be successful treatment of the disease.

Red Sox first baseman Kevin Youkilis grabs teammate Mike Lowell after the Red Sox won the game on a ninth-inning RBI double by Coco Crisp. Lowell's solo home run sparked the rally. *(Matthew West/Boston Herald)*

"It will be nice to just be treated normal and nothing special," Lester said. "I just want to go out and pitch every fifth day, and hopefully do well."

Lester left the bullpen following pregame warmups to a thunderous ovation from the capacity crowd, then seemed to struggle to control his emotions at the outset. He missed on the location of his first three pitches to Akinori Iwamura before eventually issuing a full-count walk to the Tampa Bay leadoff hitter. The lefty quickly settled his nerves, however, and struck out the next two batters before getting Pena to fly out to end the frame.

CURT SCHILLING

SCHILLING SAYS ARIZONA DELIVERED HIM TO A HIGHER LEVEL

By Rob Bradford
BOSTON HERALD
June 9, 2007

PHOENIX — Curt Schilling is coming home — again.

Phoenix has always seemed to serve as a check-post in Schilling's life. And while the street signs leading to his old home on Willow Avenue might never change, the same can't be said for the pitcher following them.

"My first night back after I was traded (from Philadelphia to Arizona on July 26, 2000), I was driving to the hotel down 32nd Street," Schilling said, "and I remember saying to myself that 17 years ago I was driving down this exact same street, and if you have had somebody driving down the exact same street 17 years later, you would say that they would never get out of this town. And to think of where I went."

The 16-year-old in that black Chevy LUV pickup truck could have never imagined that his journey out of Arizona and back again would take the route that it has.

Schilling admits that, as much as he evolved during the 14 major league seasons leading up to his initial return to his hometown in 2000, it was the three-plus seasons back in Arizona which truly defined him. And then, with the addition of his three years in Boston, you end up with the No. 38 you find today.

"What I was when I went there and what I was when I left there is two drastically different pitchers," said Schilling of his time with the Diamondbacks from 2000-03. "When I went there I had a place in the game from a reputation standpoint, and I think being part of those teams and pitching the way I pitched kind of elevated it."

When Schilling arrived in Arizona from Philadelphia — for Omar Daal, Nelson Figueroa, Travis Lee, and Vicente Padilla — he had made his mark. He hadn't had an ERA of 4.00 or higher since 1994.

But while his childhood landmarks hadn't gone anywhere upon his return, Schilling was greeted with a different kind of alteration.

He discovered that the physical challenges of a major league season demanded more of him than he had previously given. He discovered such disciplines as yoga, pilates and even martial arts, all of which certainly hadn't been on his baseball radar while attending Shadow Mountain High in Phoenix or nearby Yavapai Junior College.

"It was a point where I realized that to be in the upper half of the upper half, there's almost nothing that they do that conforms to what society does," Schilling said. "You do things dramatically different because the standard, the norm, is what everybody else does."

The change in philosophy paid dividends.

"He changed a lot," said Red Sox strength and conditioning coach Dave Page, who was with the Diamondbacks during Schilling's tenure in Arizona. "When he got to us he was 253 pounds and he pitched for us at 233 to 236. We went back in the weight room in Philadelphia and their guys were like, 'What are you doing? You didn't even know where this place was.'

"He was one guy who I looked forward to seeing every day, for a lot of reasons. He worked hard for me and he is so passionate for this craft and the industry. I love to hear him talk to young guys and just watch games with him. He taught me a lot about how to watch games. We didn't have that before he came. He kind of set our compass."

Another huge element of Schilling's metamorphosis in Arizona was the other ace on the Diamondbacks staff, Randy Johnson. The big lefty wasn't a local, having grown up in California and attended USC, and had only been with the

(Lisa Hornak/Boston Herald)

Diamondbacks since '99, but he had clearly made his mark.

It was a presence that wasn't lost on Schilling.

"It dawned on me the second day I was in Arizona, the Sunday after I pitched and saw (Johnson) pitch, that I had never been on a staff with somebody else where when they took the ball it was a win," he remembered. "In Philadelphia I had pretty much been that guy, and when you're there by yourself it's hard. All of a sudden you have some-one who totally alleviates that stress. It was unbe-lievable to watch. It was so special.

"It was a fun period of time because I grew up there. It wasn't a problem, whereas you can go home and have problems with people and time. It was a nice time. I was a very different person com-ing out of there than I was when I went there."

But as time went by during his stint in Arizona, it became clear that the next road in his baseball life was ready to be ridden. Boston would become another jumping-off point. For the kid who charted every pitch during the 1975 World Series as a 9-year-old and ate and slept the baseball simulation game APBA, the potential for a new kind of passion was perfect.

"There is nothing even close to what Sox Nation is. I am so overwhelmingly thankful that I have had the chance to experience this before my career is over," said Schilling, who has secured 30 tickets for a group that includes his former teammates from Yavapai, along with Little League coach Mike McQuaid and martial arts instructor Dr. Mike Foley, who also delivered the Schillings' first child.

"You cannot explain this and give it the due it deserves to other players," he said. "If you are a free agent, there are four or five other teams you are talking to, the dollars are somewhat comparable and Boston is one of those teams, it's a no-brainer. It's been unbelievable."

Sox pick up Lester

LEFTY SCUFFLES, BUT BATS, 'PEN SHINE

By Jeff Horrigan
BOSTON HERALD
August 22, 2007

ST. PETERSBURG, Fla. — Jon Lester reminded the Red Sox once again last night at Tropicana Field that he still needs some polish before he can shine as the gem the organization is expecting.

Coming off his best start of the season one week earlier, the 23- year-old left-hander couldn't duplicate the effort but still managed to be effective enough to defeat the Tampa Bay Devil Rays, 8-6, thanks to generous offensive support and nearly flawless relief from the bullpen.

Lester (2-0), who hadn't received a decision in his four previous outings, battled command problems and struggled to maintain a large lead but still won for the first time since defeating the Cleveland Indians in his season debut July 23. He surrendered five runs on four hits, four walks and a wild pitch in 5⅓ innings, and was touched for a pair of home runs that threatened to deprive the Sox of their ninth win in 11 meetings with the Devil Rays this season. Lester consistently worked from behind in the count and threw first-pitch strikes to only 10-of-24 batters.

"I was inconsistent once again, but luckily the bullpen picked me up and we got a win out of it, at least," said Lester, who held the Devil Rays to one run on two hits in seven innings of a no-decision August 14. "I don't know why. We've worked on some things and tried to figure it out. I think it's just a matter of pitching and going out every fifth day and getting better."

He gave up a two-run homer to Carlos Pena in the first inning that erased a 2-0 lead, and was tagged for a three-run shot by Akinori Iwamura in the fifth that turned a 7-2 advantage into a nail-biting, 7-5 edge.

Catcher Jason Varitek said he and Lester recognized his flaws and expressed confidence that the inconsistency would not be a problem in the lefty's next start Sunday in Chicago.

"I'm not going to give away what we need to do because a lot of teams pay attention," Varitek said. "We know what needs to be done better here or there to keep the excess runners off base."

Lester was provided soothing relief by Manny Delcarmen, Hideki Okajima and Jonathan Papelbon, who combined for 3⅔ hitless innings. Papelbon came on in the eighth and got four outs to become the first Sox pitcher ever to record two 30-save seasons, and the fourth closer in big league history to reach the plateau in each of his first two seasons.

"It's a huge honor for me," Papelbon said. "This was a goal I set for myself, to be a dominant closer, not just for a year but for year after year after year."

The Sox, who positioned themselves for their first three-game sweep at Tropicana Field since June 19-21, 2001, temporarily extended their AL East lead on the New York Yankees to 5 ½ games. The Bombers played late against the Los Angeles Angels in Anaheim.

Devil Rays starting pitcher Andy Sonnanstine, who ended a personal, eight-game losing streak last Wednesday at Fenway Park with 6 ⅔ solid innings (four hits, three runs), didn't come close to repeating the success this time around. The right-hander was hammered for seven runs on eight hits in five innings.

The Sox jumped out to a 2-0 lead in the first on a Kevin Youkilis double, David Ortiz triple and a Manny Ramirez sacrifice fly.

Lester, however, let the lead slip away with the two-run homer by Pena, who established a new career high with his 28th of the season.

The score remained 2-2 until the fourth, when the Sox rallied for five runs while batting around for the 32nd time this season. Varitek pushed the Sox ahead with a bases-loaded single, and Coco Crisp and Julio Lugo followed with consecutive two-run doubles that provided Lester a 7-2 lead.

Closer Jonathan Papelbon points to the final pop fly by Tampa Bay's Akinori Iwamura in the ninth inning. Papelbon became the first Red Sox to record two 30-save seasons by closing Boston's 8-6 victory. *(AP/WWP)*

BOSTON 8, TAMPA BAY 6

Clay turns his second

NO-HITS O's AFTER JUMP FROM TRIPLE-A

By Michael Silverman
BOSTON HERALD
September 2, 2007

With poise and stuff every bit the equal of Pedro Martinez and Roger Clemens on their best nights, Clay Buchholz achieved what that pair of Red Sox legends never did.

He threw a no-hitter last night.

And he is only a rookie.

In just his second major league start, the spindly 23-year-old out of Nederland, Texas, who was a 2005 supplemental draft pick, befuddled the Orioles in a 10-0 Red Sox victory, snapping the team's four-game losing streak and making Buchholz the first Red Sox rookie to throw a no-hitter.

Dazzling the Orioles lineup with an unpredictable array of baffling changeups, big-breaking curveballs and precise fastballs, Buchholz became only the third pitcher to throw a no-hitter in his first or second major league start.

Buchholz' feat was the 17th official no-hitter in Red Sox' history, the first since Derek Lowe stopped the Devil Rays on April 27, 2002.

He became the 20th rookie to throw a no-hitter and the third pitcher this season to accomplish the feat.

Buchholz walked three batters and hit another. In the ninth, Brian Roberts swung and missed at a 93-mph fastball for the first out, followed by a Corey Patterson lineout to center field. The final out came against Nick Markakis. With the count 1-2, Buchholz dropped a 77-mph curveball at Markakis' knees, a pitch so perfect that even umpire Joe West was dazzled. West waited a beat before punching out Markakis.

Catcher Jason Varitek ran to Buchholz and picked him up, starting the pig-pile. Buchholz recalls David Ortiz slapping the rookie's nose hard enough to make his eyes water.

Buchholz wasn't crying, for the pain was nothing compared to his unimaginable pleasure.

"I don't even have a word for it," said Buchholz of his emotions after the last out. "I was so excited and ecstatic about everything and the way everything boiled down to that moment and being out there. It was, you'd think we won a World Series or something, but it was an incredible moment in my life and one that I will never forget." Said owner John Henry in an e-mail: "(Red Sox chairman) Tom (Werner) and I were downstairs watching from his seats. We were both as nervous and as excited as everyone else. It was bedlam. A big win for the entire organization."

Buchholz threw 115 pitches, five shy of the limit the Sox had set in order to preserve his future, no-hit bid or not.

Thankfully, Buchholz took that decision out of the hands of manager Terry Francona.

"Somebody else might have had to put a uniform on and come take him out, because that would have been very difficult," Francona said.

As usual, Buchholz' no-hitter had its share of great defensive moments.

Second baseman Dustin Pedroia's play in the seventh, when he ranged to his right, rolled in the grass and then scrambled to his feet to throw out Miguel Tejada stood above all others.

Buchholz helped himself twice, picking off Brian Roberts in the sixth, and with his stab of a come-

Rookie pitcher Clay Buchholz waves to the Fenway Park crowd after completing a no-hitter. *(Michael Ivins/Boston Herald)*

backer from Jay Payton for the last out of the eighth. Center fielder Coco Crisp roamed the outfield with authority, hauling in six putouts.

Nearly every pitch catcher Jason Varitek called for, Buchholz was able to produce on command. As the pressure mounted in the later innings, Varitek tried not to make things more complicated.

"I wouldn't call it pressure but you don't want to put something down that is completely different," Varitek said. "You want to keep trying, thinking ahead and doing things (the same)."

The result was the stuff that legends are made of.

BOSTON 10, BALTIMORE 0

DUSTIN PEDROIA

SECOND TO NONE

By Rob Bradford
BOSTON HERALD
September 6, 2007

"When (Dustin) Pedroia gets up there and he hits a buck-fifty, discovers he can't reach the wall, and can't find his stroke because it's freezing out — well, that will happen. The rest of the organization really needs to realize this." – Red Sox general manager Theo Epstein in the book *Feeding the Monster*, talking in an organizational meeting on how patient the team might have to be with some of its young talent.

Dustin Pedroia will be the Rookie of the Year in the American League.

Doubt it? Didn't you learn your lesson the first time around?

"I always said," observed Red Sox infielder Alex Cora, "nothing against him, but his best tool is his heart. He believes."

The story of how an undersized infielder has ventured into his rookie season and performed not only better than his first-year counterparts, but better than most major leaguers is already the stuff of legend.

But understanding where Pedroia came from in managing to approach mid-September as the hard-to-argue favorite to win the league's top rookie honor lends itself to Little Leaguers' bedtime stories for years to come.

Entering May 3, Pedroia was hitting .172, the 48th-best batting average among second basemen. And now? There are just two at his position with a higher average.

The case for Pedroia stretches well beyond a casual glance. His .329 batting average (entering last night) is best among rookies and two points better than Ted Williams' rookie average (.327 in 1939). And if the season ended today, he would own the highest batting average of any rookie second baseman since 1900.

"I was always staying positive. I didn't care what people thought about me," said Pedroia, who was not in the starting lineup last night against the Blue Jays. "Everybody in the organization that had seen me in the minor leagues knew it was going to happen. I think they reminded (Red Sox manager Terry Francona) a bunch of times, and I'm glad of that."

The resilient Pedroia is the poster boy for what can happen with a little patience. But while the Red Sox are reaping the benefits of waiting for the true talent to arrive, even the organization had anxious moments that could have changed Pedroia's path to postseason honors.

"We were out in front telling people what was happening, including internally, so it kind of bought us some time," Epstein said of Pedroia's potential early struggles. "It never reached the point where we doubted his ability, but in the back of my mind I started doubting if we would run out of time with this year. If he's hitting a buck-50 in the middle of the season, you have to be concerned. We never got down on him, but at some point it would be a situation where some changes would have to be considered.

"I didn't get to that point," added Epstein of the possibility of sending Pedroia to Triple-A Pawtucket. "We talked about if we were to do that how it would help him. We kind of thought that if we did that we might lose him for the year. It wouldn't be a productive solution. It's not like sending him down would light a fire under him. It wasn't an effort question, but rather a matter of comfort."

Pedroia was probably the least concerned. Playing for the PawSox in 2006, he hit .254 in April and didn't get much better in May, improving to .263.

By the time he received the call from the Sox

in mid-August, Pedroia's average stood at .305.

"I went through something like that the year before," said the 24-year-old of his '06 season. "I didn't start hitting in Pawtucket until about 200 at-bats. I was hitting like .230, caught fire, and got over .300 like I do every year. This is just a bigger stage. I knew it was only a matter of time."

The moment the turn was finally made, according to Pedroia, came in a May 3 game at Fenway Park against Seattle. In his fourth at-bat, the rookie rifled a single into right-center field and suddenly all was right with the world.

Not only was the hit a welcome feeling for someone who hadn't had many to that point, it also showed that Pedroia couldn't be pigeon-holed into his minor league scouting report as a dead pull-hitter.

Pedroia has hit .353 since that makeup win over the Mariners, the fourth-best average in the majors. The organization's belief in Pedroia—and Francona's belief in the organization—had reaped big dividends.

The result is the best rookie in the American League.

"All the player development people said that if he struggles, he'll figure it out," Francona said. "He's a tough kid. There's more to lose than to gain by quitting on somebody. If he couldn't make it at some point . . . that obviously became a moot point at some point. But you have to stick with him, even if it isn't the popular thing to do, you have to do it."

(Matthew West/Boston Herald)

Leader of the pack

BECKETT WINS SHOWDOWN, TAKES CHARGE IN CY CHASE

By Steve Buckley
BOSTON HERALD
September 16, 2007

It was billed by many as a showdown of the American League's Cy Young Award contenders, which must have come as news to, say, Justin Verlander (17-5) and the great C.C. Sabathia (17-7).

But you know how it goes. Josh Beckett pitches for the Red Sox and Chien-Ming Wang pitches for the Yankees. A Sox-Yankees game is always guaranteed to be a headline maker anyway, whatever the names of the starting pitchers, but THIS Sox-Yankees game, played late yesterday afternoon at Fenway Park, had that added measure of sexiness that we media people — and, yes, you fans — just love.

Look at it another way: While each team has its tough-guy offensive stars — Manny Ramirez and David Ortiz for the Red Sox, Alex Rodriguez and Derek Jeter for the Yankees — can we all agree that neither of baseball's leading money-bags franchises would be in contention right now without their aces?

Josh Beckett. Chien-Ming Wang. Cy Young. Nuf Ced.

Let the record show that Beckett, improving to 19-6 with seven innings of one-run ball in the Red Sox' 10-1 victory over the Yankees, won the showdown on points, if not by the knockout that some Sox fans might have been looking for.

Remember, there is fresh, new bad blood between these teams. Yankees rookie Joba Chamberlain rode a couple of pitches up and in on Kevin Youkilis in New York a couple of weeks ago, and here was Youkilis yesterday, taking one from Wang on the wrist and having to leave the game. To add to the drama, the Red Sox' Eric Hinske plowed into Yankees catcher Jorge Posada as he was being thrown out at the plate during a three-run Boston sixth.

Beckett was bound to somehow get involved in all this. The only question was whether he'd be able to achieve the delicate balancing act of nailing somebody without getting thrown out of the game or causing his team to unravel.

He pulled it off. With two out and nobody on in the seventh inning, he threw a pitch that hit big Jason Giambi on the right side. Warnings to both sides were issued, Giambi took his base without raising a fuss, and then, after allowing a soft single to center by Robinson Cano, Beckett blew away Melky Cabrera.

The day, the game, the showdown was effectively over at that point. The Red Sox had their payback, such as it was, but what's more, they had a victory over the Yankees, ending a streak of five straight losses to their longtime rivals from the Bronx.

"He pitched like the ace of a staff today," pronounced Red Sox manager Terry Francona. "Against the best lineup in baseball he went out there and did exactly what we needed."

By "exactly what we needed," the understanding here is that what was needed was a victory, which Beckett delivered. What also was needed, perhaps, was a little gamesmanship by the Red Sox, after Youkilis was hit. And, no, Hinske barreling into Posada does not count in the payback department, since, as Beckett pointed out, "I don't

SEPTEMBER 15 VS. NEW YORK

Jacoby Ellsbury scores on a David Ortiz double in the sixth inning to put the Red Sox up 5-1. *(Matthew West/Boston Herald)*

think anybody's ever going to question Eric Hinske on how he plays the game. . . . He plays the game right. Obviously you don't want anybody to get hurt in a collision like that, but that's the right play there. I don't think anybody on their side thought that was dirty or anything. . . . Everybody that watched the game knows that was a clean deal."

OK. Fine. So then Beckett drills Giambi. Any concerns by Beckett that things might get a little crazy?

"No," Beckett said. "Everybody's just trying to grind it out. We're playing against a tough team and I'm sure they'll say the same thing. They knew they were playing against a tough team also. That's why our games usually last between 12 and 13 hours a day."

Actually, Yankees manager Joe Torre had a slightly different take on Beckett hitting Giambi.

"I am not going to comment on that," he said.

But the never-ending story that is Youkilis vs. the Yankees began Wang's unraveling. For after the apparently much-disliked (by the Yankees)

Youkilis took that Wang pitch off the wrist in the fifth inning and had to leave the game, his pinch runner, Jacoby Ellsbury, would score when J.D. Drew sliced a single to left. And in the sixth, the "pitchers' duel" aspect of this day went bye-bye, what with the Sox scoring three more runs.

"He just obviously wasn't as good as he has been lately," said Torre of Wang, who falls to 18-7 and, perhaps, out of the Cy Young race.

Cy Young? Based on what we saw yesterday, it's easy. It's Beckett.

With apologies to Justin Verlander and C.C. Sabathia.

BOSTON 10, NEW YORK 1

Sox play waiting game, then party like it's 1995

YANKS' LOSS GIVES CLUB LONG-AWAITED TITLE

By Michael Silverman
BOSTON HERALD
September 29, 2007

The grass at Fenway Park is soaking up the bubbly this morning.

Call it the breakfast of champions, cooked up by a deliriously besotted 2007 Red Sox team, which became champion of the AL East for the first time since 1995 last night.

Beginning the game against Minnesota with a magic number of two, the Red Sox solved the first-half of the equation by handling the Twins, 5-2. Then, in an absolutely surreal hour of reality TV, the Sox, along with thousands of their fans still at Fenway, watched the satellite feed of the Yankees game at Baltimore. After the Orioles rallied for three runs in the bottom of the ninth off Mariano Rivera, the Sox' clubhouse became a private sanctuary for the team, while everyone else gathered to watch the 10th inning on the super-sized video screen above the center-field bleachers. When Melvin Mora laid down the game-winner — a two-out bunt with the bases loaded — all hell broke loose and good heavens, what a party they held.

Not since 1995, when Mo Vaughn roamed the warning track atop a Boston police horse, had the Red Sox been able to declare outright ownership of the AL East. After leading the division since April 18, a stretch of 163 days, the team's grasp on first place became solid and golden in a single moment.

There are two games remaining in the regular season and a whole bunch of postseason games left in October.

For one night, though, the Red Sox could celebrate a well-earned moment.

"That was the most surreal thing ever," said manager Terry Francona, trying in vain to keep a cigar dry. "I was sitting in my office watching the game with (general manager) Theo (Epstein), John Farrell, John Henry, Tom Werner, and we were like a bunch of 13-year-olds. You've never seen a group of grown men cheering for a bunt. "We still have things to do but there's no getting around how excited we are. This is really something special, something the city can hang its hat on. We're not done, but this means a lot."

Epstein, who could not keep his grin from disappearing, carried that message, too.

"We have to sit here and enjoy it and have a good time and then compartmentalize it and move on," Epstein said. "We do have goals in mind."

Before the Bacchanalia, there was a baseball game and it featured Daisuke Matsuzaka (15-12) shutting down the Twins for eight innings, while Mike Lowell (two RBI), David Ortiz (home run), Kevin Youkilis (RBI single) and yes, J.D. Drew (RBI double) took care of business on the offensive side.

Matsuzaka, whose inconsistent outings have been maddening to some, had a breakthrough on the same night he broke the 200-inning and 200-strikeout plateaus.

Each is impressive for any rookie, but Matsuzaka was a fitting spokesman for a team that, despite its own inconsistencies, still managed to win games when it had to.

"From here there are going to be many important games in a row, and knowing that fact, I just

SEPTEMBER 28 VS. MINNESOTA

David Ortiz and a teammate spray one another with champagne as the Red Sox celebrate their first American League East title since 1995. *(Matthew West/Boston Herald)*

wanted to set myself up and throw a good game and hopefully that will carry me into the playoffs," Matsuzaka said.

If it does not, there will always be the sight of Jonathan Papelbon doing a jig by the pitcher's mound until Epstein made him stop.

The champions of one division have bigger fish to fry.

The grass at Fenway Park will dry soon enough.

The Red Sox have every intention of moistening it with bubbly exactly three more times.

BOSTON 5, MINNESOTA 2

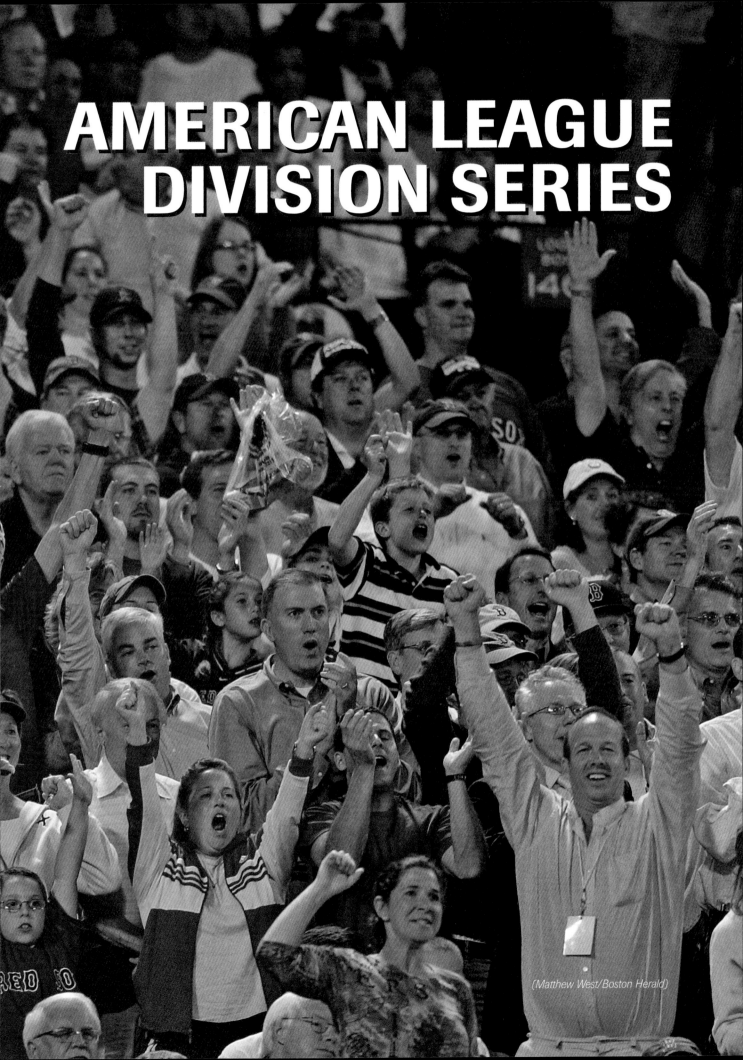

AMERICAN LEAGUE DIVISION SERIES

(Matthew West/Boston Herald)

Beckett comes up aces

STARTER'S POSTSEASON DOMINANCE
CONTINUES AS SOX TAKE OPENER

By Jeff Horrigan
BOSTON HERALD
October 4, 2007

After making New England fidget and squirm during the final month of the regular season, the Red Sox opened postseason play in a manner that allowed the region to let out a giant, pacifying exhale.

Josh Beckett pitched the franchise's first postseason shutout since Luis Tiant in Game 1 of the 1975 World Series and David Ortiz wasted no time assuming his role as October superhero, allowing the Sox to make easy work of the Los Angeles Angels with a crisp, 4-0 victory in the opener of the American League Division Series.

Pitching in the postseason for the first time since blanking the Yankees, 2-0, for the Florida Marlins in the sixth and final game of the 2003 World Series, Beckett extended his October scoreless streak to 18 innings in dominant fashion. The right-hander allowed only four singles and permitted only two runners to advance past first base, helping the Sox run their postseason winning streak against the Angels to seven games.

"Beckett was about as good as we've ever seen him," Angels manager Mike Scioscia said. "I don't think you can pitch better than that."

Beckett, who struck out eight and did not walk a batter, improved to 3-0 with a 1.36 ERA in five career starts against the Angels. Baseball's only 20-game winner effortlessly out-pitched John Lackey, one of his primary competitors for the Cy Young Award, with an effective mix of powerful fastballs, sharp curveballs and deceptive changeups.

"I never got ahead of myself," said Beckett, who became only the seventh pitcher to record back-to-back complete-

Julio Lugo reacts after being called out at second on a steal attempt to end the second inning. *(Matthew West/Boston Herald)*

ALDS GAME 1

Manny of the hour

LONGBALL CAPS HALO OF A RALLY

By Jeff Horrigan
BOSTON HERALD
October 6, 2007

The notice displayed on the center field message board in the bottom of the seventh inning, the one that said the last T would be leaving in a matter of minutes, had little effect on the largest crowd ever to attend a postseason game at Fenway Park.

With the Red Sox and Los Angeles Angels deadlocked at 3, the warning about the imminent departure of the last train home was heeded by few, leaving the ballpark packed until the very end. When all was said and done, however, scrambling to find a way home in the wee hours of the night was more than worth the hassle, considering the dramatic, unforgettable moment they witnessed after the subway stations were locked up.

Manny Ramirez crushed a three-run homer off Francisco Rodriguez over the Green Monster and onto Lansdowne Street with two outs in the bottom of the ninth inning, sending the Sox to a 6-3 victory and a commanding 2-0 lead in the American League Division Series.

Curt Schilling will attempt to complete the sweep in the best-of-five series tomorrow afternoon in Anaheim, Calif., where he squares off against Jered Weaver.

"It feels good, man," said Ramirez, who was sidelined for 24 games late in the season with a strained oblique muscle. "Sometimes I can miss three weeks and I still can come and get hits because I am one of the best players in the game. I have confidence in myself and I know my train doesn't stop there."

With the score tied at 3, Julio Lugo punched a leadoff single to left field off reliever Justin Speier (0-1) and advanced to

David Ortiz (right) and Kevin Youkilis celebrate after scoring on a J.D. Drew single in the first inning.
(Matthew West/Boston Herald)

ALDS GAME 2

BOSTON 4, LOS ANGELES 0

game shutouts in the postseason. "It was always one pitch at a time. It didn't matter what was going on. If they had a guy on third base or if they didn't have anybody on, you just go one pitch at a time."

Beckett surrendered a game-opening single up the middle to Chone Figgins before retiring the next 19 batters. Vladimir Guerrero ended the string by poking an inconsequential single to left field with one out in the seventh. The only other hits the 27-year-old allowed were a ground-ball single by Howie Kendrick in the eighth and Guerrero's bouncer up the middle in the ninth.

The 19-batter stretch matched the third-longest in postseason history, trailing only Don Larsen's perfect game in the 1956 World Series and Herb Pennock's 22-batter run in the 1927 World Series. Jim Lonborg also retired 19 straight in Game 2 of the 1967 World Series.

"He went out there today and couldn't pitch much better," said Kevin Youkilis, who clobbered a one-out home run into the Green Monster seats with one out in the first inning to give Beckett the lead.

Lackey, who won the seventh game of the 2002 World Series as a rookie, didn't pitch poorly, but he didn't come close to matching Beckett. The right-hander, who was 0-2 with an 8.38 ERA in two regular-season starts against the Sox, allowed four runs on nine hits in six innings, while striking out four and walking two.

The Sox broke the game open with a three-run rally in the third, jump-started by Youkilis' one-out double to the left field corner. Ortiz followed by smashing a thigh-high curveball into the right field seats for a two-run homer. The shot was Ortiz' ninth

Starter Josh Beckett does his best windmill impersonation while trying to field a Vladimir Guerrero single in the ninth inning. Beckett pitched a complete-game shutout. *(Matthew West/Boston Herald)*

ALDS GAME 1

career postseason homer, tying the club mark held by Jason Varitek. Manny Ramirez then walked and advanced into scoring position on a wild pitch. Mike Lowell, who was moved back to the fifth spot in the order after a month at cleanup (due to Ramirez' oblique injury), poked a full-count curve to center field for a run-scoring single.

"It's definitely great to get the first win and . . . knowing Daisuke (Matsuzaka) is going to pitch in Game 2 at home," Youkilis said.

BOSTON 4, LA ANGELS 0 • OCTOBER 3, 2007

	1	2	3	4	5	6	7	8	9		R	H	E
LA Angels	0	0	0	0	0	0	0	0	0		0	4	0
Boston	1	0	3	0	0	0	0	0	X		4	9	0

LA Angels	AB	R	H	RBI	BB	SO
Figgins, RF-CF	4	0	1	0	0	1
Cabrera, SS	4	0	0	0	0	1
Guerrero, DH	4	0	2	0	0	0
Anderson, LF	4	0	0	0	0	2
Izturis, 3B	3	0	0	0	0	0
Kotchman, 1B	3	0	0	0	0	1
Kendrick, 2B	3	0	1	0	0	0
Napoli, C	2	0	0	0	0	1
a-Aybar, PH-RF	1	0	0	0	0	0
Willits, CF	2	0	0	0	0	1
b-Morales, PH	1	0	0	0	0	1
Mathis, C	0	0	0	0	0	0
Totals	31	0	4	0	0	8

a-Grounded into a forceout for Napoli in the 8th. b-Struck out for Willits in the 8th.

BATTING
Team LOB: 4.

FIELDING
DP: 3 (Kendrick-Kotchman, Kendrick-Cabrera-Kotchman, Kotchman-Cabrera-Lackey).

PITCHING

LA Angels	IP	H	R	ER	BB	SO	HR
Lackey (L, 0-1)	6.0	9	4	4	2	4	2
Santana	2.0	0	0	0	0	2	0

Boston	AB	R	H	RBI	BB	SO
Pedroia, 2B	4	0	0	0	0	1
Youkilis, 1B	4	2	2	1	0	1
Ortiz, DH	3	1	2	2	1	0
Ramirez, LF	3	1	1	0	1	1
Ellsbury, LF	0	0	0	0	0	0
Lowell, 3B	3	0	1	1	0	0
Drew, RF	3	0	1	0	0	0
Varitek, C	3	0	1	0	0	1
Crisp, CF	3	0	0	0	0	0
Lugo, SS	3	0	1	0	0	2
Totals	29	4	9	4	2	6

BATTING
2B: Youkilis (1, Lackey).
HR: Youkilis (1, 1st inning off Lackey, 0 on, 1 out), Ortiz (1, 3rd inning off Lackey, 1 on, 1 out).
Team LOB: 3.

BASERUNNING
CS: Lugo (1, 2nd base by Lackey/Napoli).

PITCHING

Boston	IP	H	R	ER	BB	SO	HR
Beckett (W, 1-0)	9.0	4	0	0	0	8	0

Manny of the hour

LONGBALL CAPS HALO OF A RALLY

By Jeff Horrigan
BOSTON HERALD
October 6, 2007

The notice displayed on the center field message board in the bottom of the seventh inning, the one that said the last T would be leaving in a matter of minutes, had little effect on the largest crowd ever to attend a postseason game at Fenway Park.

With the Red Sox and Los Angeles Angels deadlocked at 3, the warning about the imminent departure of the last train home was heeded by few, leaving the ballpark packed until the very end. When all was said and done, however, scrambling to find a way home in the wee hours of the night was more than worth the hassle, considering the dramatic, unforgettable moment they witnessed after the subway stations were locked up.

Manny Ramirez crushed a three-run homer off Francisco Rodriguez over the Green Monster and onto Lansdowne Street with two outs in the bottom of the ninth inning, sending the Sox to a 6-3 victory and a commanding 2-0 lead in the American League Division Series.

Curt Schilling will attempt to complete the sweep in the best-of-five series tomorrow afternoon in Anaheim, Calif., where he squares off against Jered Weaver.

"It feels good, man," said Ramirez, who was sidelined for 24 games late in the season with a strained oblique muscle. "Sometimes I can miss three weeks and I still can come and get hits because I am one of the best players in the game. I have confidence in myself and I know my train doesn't stop there."

With the score tied at 3, Julio Lugo punched a leadoff single to left field off reliever Justin Speier (0-1) and advanced to

David Ortiz (right) and Kevin Youkilis celebrate after scoring on a J.D. Drew single in the first inning.
(Matthew West/Boston Herald)

ALDS GAME 2

Left fielder Manny Ramirez misplays a ball hit by the Angels' Chone Figgins in the second inning. Figgins' double drove in a run as Los Angeles took a 3-2 lead in the inning. *(Matt Stone/Boston Herald)*

second on Dustin Pedroia's broken-bat groundout. Angels manager Mike Scioscia then called on closer Rodriguez, who struck out Kevin Youkilis before issuing an intentional walk to David Ortiz.

That brought up Ramirez, who was 0-for-2 with a pair of walks to that point. The left fielder clobbered a 96 mph fastball over the promotional cola bottles on the light tower, sending the place into absolute bedlam.

"It's one of the best feelings ever," Ramirez said of his first walkoff HR with the Red Sox. "You know I never look for pitches. I always trust myself. In that situation, that guy got me out so many times. But

baseball's like that. Sometimes you get me, sometimes I get you. And I got him at the right time."

Added Scioscia: "Well, you really pick your poison. We're going to take our chances with some matchups. It just made sense not to go after David, and it didn't work tonight.

The shot was the ninth postseason walkoff hit in Sox history and the first since Ortiz' game-winning, 14th-inning single against New York in Game 5 of the 2004 AL Championship Series. It was the fifth walkoff homer in club history and the first since Ortiz' 12th-inning shot off Yankees reliever Paul Quantrill in Game 4 of the 2004 ALCS.

ALDS GAME 2

Two nights after Josh Beckett dominated the Angels with a four-hit shutout in Game 1, Sox starter Daisuke Matsuzaka lasted only 4⅔ innings, allowing three runs on seven hits and three walks before being lifted with a 3-2 deficit in the fifth. Matsuzaka, who made a name for himself as a big-game pitcher in international competition, was provided a 2-0 lead in the first, only to quickly let it slip away in the Angels' three-run second. The Sox tied things at 3 in the fifth on Mike Lowell's bases-loaded sacrifice fly.

Their bullpen held it there, with Javier Lopez, Manny Delcarmen, Hideki Okajima and Jonathan Papelbon (1-0) combining on 4 ⅓ hitless innings of relief.

BOSTON 6, LA ANGELS 3 • OCTOBER 5, 2007

	1	2	3	4	5	6	7	8	9	R	H	E
LA Angels	0	3	0	0	0	0	0	0	0	3	7	0
Boston	2	0	0	0	1	0	0	0	3	6	6	1

LA Angels	AB	R	H	RBI	BB	SO
Figgins, CF-RF	5	1	1	1	0	3
Cabrera, SS	4	0	1	1	1	0
Guerrero, RF	3	0	0	0	0	0
Napoli, C	1	0	0	0	0	0
Anderson, LF	4	0	2	0	1	0
Izturis, 3B	5	0	1	0	0	2
Kotchman, 1B	2	1	0	0	2	0
Morales, DH	4	1	1	0	0	1
Kendrick, 2B	4	0	1	0	0	1
Mathis, C	3	0	0	1	0	0
a-Rivera, PH	0	0	0	0	1	0
1-Willits, PR-CF	0	0	0	0	0	0
Totals	35	3	7	3	5	7

a-Walked for Mathis in the 8th.
1-Ran for Rivera in the 8th.

BATTING
2B: Figgins (1, Matsuzaka), Cabrera (1, Matsuzaka), Anderson (1, Matsuzaka).
Team LOB: 11.

BASERUNNING
SB: Izturis 2 (2, 2nd base off Matsuzaka/Varitek, 2nd base off Matsuzaka/Varitek), Willits (1, 2nd base off Papelbon/Varitek), Kendrick 2 (2, 2nd base off Papelbon/Varitek, 3rd base off Papelbon/Varitek).

FIELDING
Outfield assists: Figgins (Crisp at 1st base).
DP: (Figgins-Kotchman-Kendrick).

PITCHING

LA Angels	IP	H	R	ER	BB	SO	HR
Escobar	5.0	4	3	3	5	5	0
Shields	2.0	0	0	0	3	1	0
Speier (L, 0-1)	1.1	1	1	1	0	0	0
Rodriguez, F	0.1	1	2	2	1	1	1

Boston	AB	R	H	RBI	BB	SO
Pedroia, 2B	5	1	1	0	0	0
Youkilis, 1B	4	1	0	0	1	2
Ortiz, DH	1	2	1	0	4	0
Ramirez, LF	3	1	1	3	2	1
Lowell, 3B	2	0	0	1	1	0
Drew, RF	4	0	1	2	0	0
Varitek, C	4	0	0	0	0	1
Crisp, CF	3	0	1	0	1	1
Lugo, SS	4	1	1	0	0	2
Totals	30	6	6	6	9	7

BATTING
2B: Pedroia (1, Escobar).
HR: Ramirez (1, 9th inning off Rodriguez, F, 2 on, 2 out).
Team LOB: 8.

BASERUNNING
SB: Crisp (1, 2nd base off Escobar/Mathis).

FIELDING
E: Lowell (1, throw).

PITCHING

Boston	IP	H	R	ER	BB	SO	HR
Matsuzaka	4.2	7	3	3	3	3	0
Lopez	0.1	0	0	0	0	0	0
Delcarmen	1.1	0	0	0	0	1	0
Okajima	1.1	0	0	0	0	2	0
Papelbon (W, 1-0)	1.1	0	0	0	2	1	0

BOSTON 6, LOS ANGELES 3

Sox look heaven sent

SCHILLING HURLS TEAM INTO ALCS

By Michael Silverman
BOSTON HERALD
October 8, 2007

ANAHEIM, Calif. – It wasn't even close.

It almost wasn't fair.

The Red Sox are going to the American League Championship Series for the third time in the last five years, after completing a three-game sweep of the listless Los Angeles Angels with a 9-1 victory.

Getting big games from their biggest names – Curt Schilling threw seven scoreless innings, while David Ortiz and Manny Ramirez hit back-to-back home runs – the Red Sox put the last coat of shellack on a three-game masterpiece, in which they dominated the Angels in every facet of the game.

The Sox lineup outscored (19-4), outhomered (5-0) and outslugged (.495 to .253) the Angels in the series, and the pitchers also outdid their counterparts, from the starters' ERA (1.31 to 5.06) to batting-average against (.192 to .269).

"We have to give credit to our pitching staff for getting those guys out the whole series," said general manager Theo Epstein, a couple of seconds before getting drenched by a Ramirez-wielded bucket of ice water.

Ramirez' second home run in as many games came just after Ortiz had stroked his second home run of the series, in the fourth inning off of Jered Weaver.

The 2-0 lead held until the eighth, when the rest of the offense got in on the act with a seven-run outburst that sent the Southern California fans scurrying home.

"I think in big games like this you need your big guys to come through," Mike Lowell (2-for-4, RBI double) said. "And (Ramirez and Ortiz) do, time and time again. . . . I think those two basically set the tone of all three games of the series with

Designated hitter David Ortiz points skyward after hitting his fourth-inning home run. Ortiz was 2-3 in Boston's series-clinching 9-1 victory.
(Matthew West/Boston Herald)

ALDS GAME 3

BOSTON 9, LOS ANGELES 1

Closer Jonathan Papelbon sprays champagne in the clubhouse after the Boston Red Sox complete their ALDS sweep of the Los Angeles Angels. *(Matthew West/Boston Herald)*

their bats. And that's why they're superstars."

Schilling pitched as one would expect him to come October. There was seldom a perilous situation for him to work out of, save for a two-out, bases-loaded jam in the third, which ended with Reggie Willits harmlessly fouling out to catcher Jason Varitek. Schilling struck out four, allowed six hits and walked just one.

"Schilling executed a great pitch to get out of that (third-inning) jam," manager Terry Francona said. "A base hit, we're (tied at) 2-2, or a ball in the gap and we're losing."

After this drubbing, it seems almost impossible to imagine a scenario in which the Red Sox could have lost. The Angels were hit hard by injuries — Gary Matthews Jr. was a scratch before the series, Garret Anderson was bothered all series by conjunctivitis — and were never in a position to implement their slash-and-dash, run-manufacturing offense.

To have Schilling complete the one-sided affair only made the day sweeter for the Red Sox.

"He was carving on both sides of the plate," said Epstein. "It's so hard to execute perfection with that kind of command pitch after pitch, and he really did it. He was really an artist."

ALDS GAME 3

In the end, another wet-and-wild postgame celebration did nothing but drive home how well this team is playing.

"It surprised me that we played this (well) and (had) everything come together," said principal owner John Henry. "Those three pitchers (Game 1 starter Josh Beckett, Game 2 starter Daisuke Matsuzaka and Schilling) and the great bullpen — we only gave up four runs. And we were flawless defensively. After 162 games, you know that anything can happen in a short series."

That's true. But with the Sox playing this well, it now seems like this is the only way this series could've ended.

BOSTON 9, LA ANGELS 1 • OCTOBER 7, 2007

	1	2	3	4	5	6	7	8	9		R	H	E
Boston	0	0	0	2	0	0	0	7	0		9	10	0
LA Angels	0	0	0	0	0	0	0	0	1		1	8	0

Boston	AB	R	H	RBI	BB	SO
Pedroia, 2B	4	1	1	1	1	1
Youkilis, 1B	4	0	1	1	0	1
Ortiz, DH	3	2	2	1	1	1
a-Hinske, PH-DH	1	0	0	0	0	1
Ramirez, LF	2	1	1	1	2	0
1-Ellsbury, PR-LF	1	1	0	0	0	0
Lowell, 3B	4	1	2	1	0	0
Drew, RF	4	1	0	1	0	1
Varitek, C	4	1	1	1	0	2
Crisp, CF	4	0	1	2	0	2
Lugo, SS	3	1	1	0	1	0
Totals	**34**	**9**	**10**	**9**	**5**	**9**

a-Struck out for Ortiz in the 9th.
1-Ran for Ramirez in the 8th.

BATTING
2B: Lowell 2 (2, Weaver, Speier), Pedroia (2, Speier), Varitek (1, Oliver).
HR: Ortiz (2, 4th inning off Weaver, 0 on, 0 out), Ramirez (2, 4th inning off Weaver, 0 on, 0 out).
Team LOB: 4.

BASERUNNING
SB: Lugo (1, 2nd base off Weaver/Napoli).

FIELDING
DP: (Lugo-Pedroia-Youkilis).

PITCHING

Boston	IP	H	R	ER	BB	SO	HR
Schilling (W, 1-0)	7.0	6	0	0	1	4	0
Okajima	1.0	1	0	0	1	0	0
Gagne	1.0	1	1	1	0	1	0

LA Angels	AB	R	H	RBI	BB	SO
Figgins, CF	4	0	1	0	0	0
Cabrera, SS	4	0	2	0	0	0
Guerrero, RF	3	0	0	0	1	0
Anderson, LF	1	0	0	0	0	0
Willits, LF	2	0	0	0	1	1
Morales, 1B	4	0	0	0	0	0
Izturis, 3B	4	1	3	0	0	0
Kendrick, 2B	3	0	0	1	0	0
Rivera, DH	3	0	1	0	0	1
a-Haynes, PH-DH	1	0	0	0	0	1
Napoli, C	3	0	1	0	0	2
b-Quinlan, PH	1	0	0	0	0	0
Totals	**33**	**1**	**8**	**1**	**2**	**5**

a-Struck out for Rivera in the 9th. b-Flied out for Napoli in the 9th.

BATTING
2B: Izturis 2 (2, Schilling, Gagne), Figgins (2, Okajima).
Team LOB: 8.

FIELDING
DP: 3 (Kendrick-Morales, Cabrera-Kendrick-Morales, Kendrick-Morales-Cabrera-Kendrick).

PITCHING

LA Angels	IP	H	R	ER	BB	SO	HR
Weaver (L, 0-1)	5.0	4	2	2	3	5	2
Shields	2.0	0	1	1	1	3	0
Speier	0.1	3	4	4	1	0	0
Oliver	0.2	2	2	2	0	0	0
Moseley	1.0	1	0	0	0	1	0

BOSTON 9, LOS ANGELES 1

AMERICAN LEAGUE CHAMPIONSHIP SERIES

Beckett lone pitcher to show up for duel

RAMIREZ, ORTIZ LEAD SOX IN SERIES-OPENING BLOWOUT

By Jeff Horrigan
BOSTON HERALD
October 13, 2007

It turned out that only one of the weapons was loaded in the anticipated pitching duel between Josh Beckett and C.C. Sabathia last night.

The matchup between the top contenders for the American League Cy Young Award was as one-sided as the set on a Hollywood soundstage, with Beckett completely out-pitching Sabathia, enabling the Red Sox to pound the Cleveland Indians, 10-3, in Game 1 of the AL Championship Series at Fenway Park.

The only 20-game winner in the majors this season, Beckett followed up on his masterful performance in the first game of the Division Series by allowing only two runs on four hits in six innings, while striking out seven.

"When you're facing a guy like C.C. . . . you'd better have somebody you believe in and we do, because you're going to have to beat really good pitchers to keep moving on," Sox manager Terry Francona said.

David Ortiz and Manny Ramirez keyed the offensive onslaught by reaching base 10 times. The Nos. 3-4 hitters combined for four hits, five walks and a hit batsman. Ortiz has reached base safely in 16-of-18 plate appearances in the post-season, while Ramirez has done so in 11 of his last 12 trips to the plate.

"I've never seen anything like it," No. 5 hitter Mike Lowell (1-for-3, two-run double, sacrifice fly, walk) said. "They're unbelievable."

Josh Beckett pitches to the Indians in the first inning of Game 1.
(Stuart Cahill/Boston Herald)

ALCS GAME 1

BOSTON 10, CLEVELAND 3

Manny Ramirez makes a diving, er, rolling catch on an Asdrubal Cabrera fly ball in the eighth inning. *(Matthew West/Boston Herald)*

Sabathia, second to Beckett with 19 wins, fired blanks throughout his disastrous, 4⅓-inning outing. The hulking left-hander was hammered for eight runs on seven hits, five walks and a hit batsman, allowing the Sox to move within three wins of the World Series.

"He didn't have it tonight," Indians manager Eric Wedge said of his ace. "His command was off. He was off a little bit with his fastball, having trouble getting his breaking ball where he needed to. He was running away from his changeup a little bit. He just never really got in sync."

Beckett struck out the first two batters he faced before leaving a belt-high fastball over the heart of the plate to Travis Hafner, who smashed it into the visitors bullpen for a 1-0 Cleveland lead. The Sox ace was unfazed. He retired the next 10 Indians, as well as 11 of the next 12, before allowing a two-out double to Kenny Lofton in the fifth inning.

As was the case when he shut out Los Angeles in Game 1 of the Division Series, Beckett had all of his pitches working last night. He confounded Cleveland with a blazing fastball, sharp curveball and deceptive changeup. Five of the seven strike-outs came via two-strike curves; one apiece on the fastball and change.

Sabathia immediately gave the run back in the home half of the first inning on successive, one-out singles by Kevin Youkilis, Ortiz and Ramirez, then

ALCS GAME 1

displayed a flash of his regular-season brilliance by striking out the side in the second.

But he lost all effectiveness in the third, when the Sox sent nine men to the plate in a four-run rally.

Julio Lugo started things off by punching a leadoff double to right field. Sabathia proceeded to load the bases with one out by issuing a walk to Kevin Youkilis and hitting Ortiz with a pitch, then forced in a run by walking Ramirez after getting ahead in the count 0-2. Lowell followed with a two-run, opposite-field double, Bobby Kielty was intentionally walked to load the bases and Jason Varitek

pushed across the fifth Sox run with a fielder's choice chopper to third.

The Sox broke open the game in the fifth after Sabathia again loaded the bases. Kielty's two-run single to right made it 7-1 and ended Sabathia's evening. Varitek greeted reliever Jensen Lewis with a run-scoring double to right-center to extend the lead to 8-1.

Beckett allowed the Indians a second run in the sixth on two hits, but the Sox scored a pair in the same inning to put the game out of reach before the bullpen door opened.

BOSTON 10, CLEVELAND 3 • OCTOBER 12, 2007

	1	2	3	4	5	6	7	8	9		R	H	E
Cleveland	1	0	0	0	0	1	0	1	0		3	8	0
Boston	1	0	4	0	3	2	0	0	X		10	12	0

Cleveland	AB	R	H	RBI	BB	SO
Sizemore, CF	5	0	0	0	0	3
Cabrera, 2B	3	0	1	2	0	1
Hafner, DH	3	1	1	1	1	1
Martinez, C	4	0	0	0	0	1
Garko, 1B	2	0	1	0	0	0
a-Gomez, PH	1	0	0	0	0	1
Peralta, SS	4	0	1	0	0	0
Lofton, LF	4	0	2	0	0	1
Gutierrez, RF	4	0	0	0	0	3
Blake, 3B	3	2	2	0	1	0
Totals	33	3	8	3	2	11

a-Struck out for Garko in the 9th.

BATTING
2B: Lofton 2 (2, Beckett, Gagne), Blake 2 (2, Beckett, Lopez).
HR: Hafner (1, 1st inning off Beckett, 0 on, 2 out).
Team LOB: 7.

FIELDING
Outfield assists: Gutierrez (Lowell at 3rd base).
DP: (Cabrera-Peralta-Garko).

PITCHING

Cleveland	IP	H	R	ER	BB	SO	HR
Sabathia (L, 0-1)	4.1	7	8	8	5	3	0
Lewis	0.2	3	2	2	0	0	0
Fultz	0.0	0	0	0	2	0	0
Mastny	2.0	1	0	0	0	2	0
Borowski	1.0	1	0	0	1	0	0

Boston	AB	R	H	RBI	BB	SO
Pedroia, 2B	4	1	1	0	0	1
Youkilis, 1B	4	3	2	0	1	0
Ortiz, DH	2	2	2	0	2	0
Ramirez, LF	2	2	2	3	3	0
1-Ellsbury, PR-LF	0	0	0	0	0	0
Lowell, 3B	3	0	1	3	1	0
Kielty, RF	2	1	1	2	1	1
a-Drew, PH-RF	2	0	0	0	0	0
Varitek, C	5	0	1	2	0	2
Crisp, CF	4	0	1	0	0	1
Lugo, SS	4	1	1	0	0	0
Totals	32	10	12	10	8	5

a-Flied out for Kielty in the 6th.
1-Ran for Ramirez in the 8th.

BATTING
2B: Lugo (1, Sabathia), Lowell (1, Sabathia), Varitek (1, Lewis), Crisp (1, Mastny), Ortiz (1, Borowski).
Team LOB: 9.

FIELDING
DP: (Lugo-Pedroia-Youkilis).

PITCHING

Boston	IP	H	R	ER	BB	SO	HR
Beckett (W, 1-0)	6.0	4	2	2	0	7	1
Timlin	1.0	1	0	0	0	1	0
Lopez	1.0	1	1	1	1	0	0
Gagne	1.0	2	0	0	1	3	0

BOSTON 10, CLEVELAND 3

Bullpen opens a 7-11

NO RELIEF FOR GAGNE, SOX AS INDIANS EVEN SERIES

By Michael Silverman
BOSTON HERALD
October 14, 2007

Pressed into heavy duty just once in the previous four postseason games, the Red Sox bullpen came down with a severe case of battle fatigue at the end of Game 2 of the ALCS last night against Cleveland.

The first three relievers — Manny Delcarmen, Hideki Okajima and Jonathan Papelbon — had come through like aces for the most part in the first $5\frac{1}{3}$ innings of relief, allowing a single run.

The final trio of Eric Gagne, Javier Lopez and Jon Lester, however, managed to triple-handedly convert a 6-6 game into a 13-6 Indians victory.

"It kind of just snowballed," said Lester. "We didn't do the job we came in there to do. I sure didn't help out. That was unacceptable."

The entire top of the 11th was a bit unbelievable, as well.

It had begun innocently enough with a Gagne strikeout, but seven of the next eight batters reached base. Gagne, who had already left the Red Sox clubhouse before the media was allowed in last night, allowed a single and a walk, Lopez allowed two RBI hits and uncorked a wild pitch that brought in a run, while Lester allowed an RBI double and a three-run home run to Franklin Gutierrez that rubbed salt on everyone's wounded pride.

"It's very disappointing," said Lopez. "We had battled all game long, the lead going back and forth, back and forth. We had some good momentum going there with Papelbon throwing quality innings and Okajima settled things down. It's just unfortunate it ended the way it did."

With Dustin Pedroia looking on, David Ortiz slides in safely to score on a Mike Lowell hit in the third inning. *(John Wilcox/Boston Herald)*

ALCS GAME 2

CLEVELAND 13, BOSTON 6

Red Sox shortstop Julio Lugo chases down Ryan Garko's fourth-inning single. *(Matthew West/Boston Herald)*

Up until then, the story of the Red Sox bullpen story was going to be a happy one.

Despite a single run allowed by Delcarmen in the sixth that tied the game at 6, the bullpen had done what was asked — keep the game close for 5⅓ innings and allow the Red Sox offense enough time to do what it could, which wound up being nothing.

Okajima came into the game in relief in the sixth inning, just after Delcarmen had allowed a walk, a single and then an RBI groundout. Okajima's first order of business was to retire No. 9 hitter Casey Blake on a strikeout. Okajima allowed an infield hit before Travis Hafner lined out to second baseman Dustin Pedroia, who was perfectly positioned in shallow right field.

ALCS GAME 2

Okajima was stronger in the seventh, retiring the side in order. Timlin, left unused in the ALDS after allowing no runs in his final four appearances of the regular season, delivered a top-notch inning of relief in the eighth, retiring the bottom third of the Indians lineup in order.

Papelbon was in near-dominating form in the ninth. He retired the first two batters, allowed a single, then walked a batter intentionally before getting the necessary fielder's choice groundout.

In the top of the 10th, Papelbon retired the side in order.

Then, there was the 11th.

"You know, both us and Cleveland had gotten into our bullpens so early and our bullpens really did a pretty good job, getting to extra innings," Francona said. "You're trying to stop one run and the bottom kind of fell out for us."

CLEVELAND 13, BOSTON 6 • OCTOBER 13, 2007

	1	2	3	4	5	6	7	8	9	10	11	R	H	E
Cleveland	1	0	0	3	1	1	0	0	0	0	7	13	17	0
Boston	0	0	3	0	3	0	0	0	0	0	0	6	10	0

Cleveland	AB	R	H	RBI	BB	SO
Sizemore, CF	5	3	3	1	1	0
Cabrera, 2B	5	1	1	0	1	1
Hafner, DH	5	0	2	0	0	0
1-Barfield, PR-DH	0	0	0	0	0	0
a-Nixon, PH-DH	1	0	1	1	0	0
2-Michaels, PR-DH	0	1	0	0	0	0
Martinez, C	4	2	3	1	2	1
Garko, 1B	6	2	2	1	0	0
Peralta, SS	5	3	3	4	1	2
Lofton, LF	6	0	1	0	0	0
Gutierrez, RF	6	1	1	4	0	1
Blake, 3B	6	0	0	0	0	4
Totals	49	13	17	12	5	9

Boston	AB	R	H	RBI	BB	SO
Pedroia, 2B	4	1	1	0	1	2
1-Ellsbury, PR	0	0	0	0	0	0
Cora, 2B	0	0	0	0	0	0
Youkilis, 1B	4	0	1	0	1	1
Ortiz, DH	4	2	1	0	1	0
Ramirez, LF	4	1	1	3	1	1
Lowell, 3B	5	1	2	3	0	1
Drew, RF	5	0	2	0	0	0
Varitek, C	5	0	0	0	0	2
Crisp, CF	5	1	2	0	0	1
Lugo, SS	4	0	0	0	1	2
Totals	40	6	10	6	5	10

a-Singled for Barfield in the 11th.
1-Ran for Hafner in the 9th. 2-Ran for Nixon in the 11th.

BATTING
2B: Sizemore (1, Schilling), Martinez (1, Schilling), Peralta (1, Lester).
HR: Peralta (1, 4th inning off Schilling, 2 on, 1 out), Sizemore (1, 5th inning off Schilling, 0 on, 1 out), Gutierrez (1, 11th inning off Lester, 2 on, 2 out).
Team LOB: 8.

BASERUNNING
SB: Barfield (1, 2nd base off Papelbon/Varitek).

FIELDING
DP: 3 (Blake-Cabrera-Garko, Peralta-Cabrera-Garko 2).

PITCHING

Cleveland	IP	H	R	ER	BB	SO	HR
Carmona	4.0	4	4	4	5	5	0
Perez	0.1	3	2	2	0	0	2
Lewis	2.1	0	0	0	0	1	0
Betancourt	2.1	1	0	0	0	3	0
Mastny (W, 1-0)	1.0	0	0	0	0	0	0
Borowski	1.0	2	0	0	0	1	0

1-Ran for Pedroia in the 9th.

BATTING
HR: Ramirez (1, 5th inning off Perez, 1 on, 1 out), Lowell (1, 5th inning off Perez, 0 on, 1 out).
Team LOB: 6.

BASERUNNING
SB: Ellsbury (1, 2nd base off Betancourt/Martinez), Crisp (1, 2nd base off Carmona/Martinez).

FIELDING
DP: (Lugo-Pedroia-Youkilis).

PITCHING

Boston	IP	H	R	ER	BB	SO	HR
Schilling	4.2	9	5	5	0	3	2
Delcarmen	0.2	1	1	1	1	0	0
Okajima	1.2	1	0	0	1	3	0
Timlin	1.0	0	0	0	0	0	0
Papelbon	2.0	1	0	0	1	1	0
Gagne (L, 0-1)	0.1	1	2	2	1	1	0
Lopez	0.0	2	3	3	1	0	0
Lester	0.2	2	2	2	0	1	1

Dice-K, Sox fizzle again

SHOW LITTLE POP VS. WESTBROOK

By Michael Silverman
BOSTON HERALD
October 16, 2007

CLEVELAND — There will be no bubbly in Cleveland this time.

When the Red Sox came to Cleveland in October 1999, they left the visitors clubhouse a champagne-soaked, cigar-stenched mess after their five-game American League Division Series win.

The clubhouse will be dry this time around after the Indians' 4-2 victory in Game 3 last night. Now it is Cleveland, up 2-1 in the AL Championship Series, that is just two wins away from celebrating a series victory on its home turf and moving on to the World Series.

Nobody was expecting the Daisuke Matsuzaka-Jake Westbrook matchup to result in a low-scoring pitchers' duel, but only Matsuzaka held up his end of that assumption. Allowing four runs on six hits in $4\frac{2}{3}$ innings, Matsuzaka's effort was an even bigger disappointment than his $4\frac{2}{3}$-inning stint in Game 2 of the AL Division Series against the Angels. He at least got the no-decision in that one, but now he is the poster child for the hole in which the Red Sox find themselves.

Matsuzaka allowed Kenny Lofton's two-run home run in the second inning, then two more runs in the fifth, when five batters in a row reached base on four singles and a walk.

Westbrook was close to unhittable, the Red Sox only getting to him in the seventh when Jason Varitek hit a one-out, two-run home run to center.

When the Red Sox did reach base against Westbrook, they wasted numerous opportunities, including a bases-loaded, no-out threat in the second inning.

All eyes were on Daisuke Matsuzaka after he gave up a two-run home run in the second inning of Game 3. *(Stuart Cahill/Boston Herald)*

ALCS GAME 3

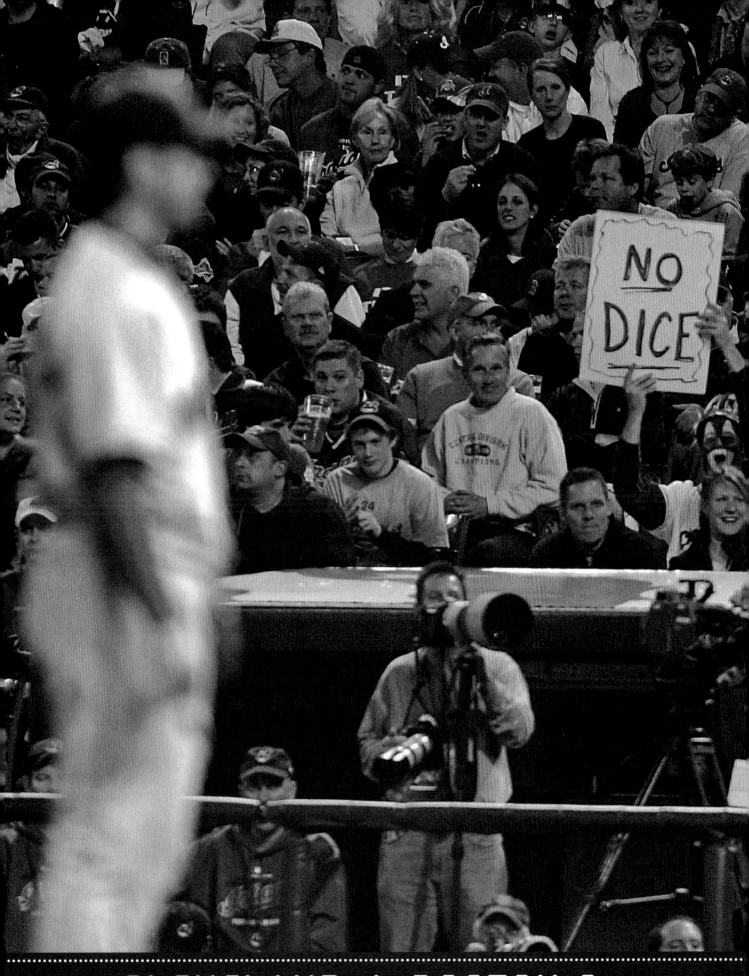

CLEVELAND 4, BOSTON 2

Dustin Pedroia throws to first after forcing out Cleveland's Alex Cora in the fifth inning. *(John Wilcox/Boston Herald)*

"We've been here before, down 2-1," said Varitek, who thought Matsuzaka pitched better last night than he did against the Angels. "This team needs to keep battling and play good baseball. I'm confident in the whole team."

Matsuzaka appeared to be sinking into a deep spiral of despair and dismay the longer he sat staring into his locker after the game. While the media awaited his decision to speak or not, Matsuzaka muttered to himself, looked up at the ceiling and softly pounded his fist against his forehead.

Finally, he issued the following through his translator, Masa Hoshino.

"As you saw I allowed them to score first and I wasn't able to hang on after giving up the lead," Matsuzaka said. "I wanted to do everything I could today to win and hand it over to (tonight's starter Tim) Wakefield in a good way."

Matsuzaka could not do that, and the Red Sox had their second poor start in a row to beat themselves up about as this series enters a new stage of drama tonight.

ALCS GAME 3

Wakefield will square off against an Indians line-up that in the past two games has seemed more and more capable of delivering the kind of clutch hits the Red Sox are not collecting. The mush-tossing Paul Byrd starts for the Indians, and if anybody saw his masterful effort against the Yankees in the Division Series, they will understand he is no pushover.

Westbrook certainly came up with a sterling start. Keeping the Red Sox on their heels by repeatedly throwing first-pitch strikes – he got ahead 0-1 on 21 of the 27 batters he faced, with 15 called strikes – he provided the best start yet from an Indians pitching staff that has not benefited from

the pair of aces, C.C. Sabathia and Fausto Carmona, atop the rotation.

"We hit some balls good, but we have nothing to show for it," said Dustin Pedroia, who put up an 0-for-4 effort with two strikeouts.

The nothing-to-show-for-it Red Sox will get every chance to play catch-up tonight. If they can, last night's effort will fade away somewhat.

If the team cannot get it done again tonight, then this game will go down as a loss all the Red Sox, not just Matsuzaka, will beat themselves up about again and again for a long time.

CLEVELAND 4, BOSTON 2 • OCTOBER 15, 2007

	1	2	3	4	5	6	7	8	9	R	H	E
Boston	0	0	0	0	0	0	2	0	0	2	7	0
Cleveland	0	2	0	0	2	0	0	0	X	4	6	1

Boston	AB	R	H	RBI	BB	SO
Pedroia, 2B	4	0	0	0	0	2
Youkilis, 1B	3	0	1	0	1	1
Ortiz, DH	3	0	1	0	1	0
Ramirez, LF	3	0	1	0	1	0
Lowell, 3B	4	0	1	0	0	0
Drew, RF	4	1	1	0	0	0
Varitek, C	4	1	1	2	0	0
Crisp, CF	3	0	0	0	0	1
Lugo, SS	3	0	1	0	0	0
Totals	**31**	**2**	**7**	**2**	**3**	**4**

BATTING
2B: Ortiz (2, Westbrook).
HR: Varitek (1, 7th inning off Westbrook, 1 on, 1 out).
Team LOB: 5.

PITCHING
Boston	IP	H	R	ER	BB	SO	HR
Matsuzaka (L, 0-1)	4.2	6	4	4	2	6	1
Timlin	1.1	0	0	0	0	2	0
Okajima	1.1	0	0	0	1	0	0
Delcarmen	0.2	0	0	0	0	2	0

Cleveland	AB	R	H	RBI	BB	SO
Sizemore, CF	3	1	0	0	1	0
Cabrera, 2B	4	0	2	1	0	1
Hafner, DH	3	0	0	1	1	1
Martinez, C	3	0	1	0	1	1
Garko, 1B	4	1	1	0	0	2
Peralta, SS	4	0	0	0	0	3
Lofton, LF	3	1	1	2	0	1
Nixon, RF	3	0	0	0	0	1
Gutierrez, RF	0	0	0	0	0	0
Blake, 3B	3	1	1	0	0	0
Totals	30	4	6	4	3	10

BATTING
HR: Lofton (1, 2nd inning off Matsuzaka, 1 on, 2 out).
Team LOB: 5.

FIELDING
E: Garko (1, fielding).
DP: 3 (Cabrera-Blake-Garko, Peralta-Cabrera-Garko, Peralta-Garko).

PITCHING
Cleveland	IP	H	R	ER	BB	SO	HR
Westbrook (W, 1-0)	6.2	7	2	2	3	2	1
Lewis (H, 1)	0.1	0	0	0	0	1	0
Betancourt (H, 1)	1.0	0	0	0	0	1	0
Borowski (S, 1)	1.0	0	0	0	0	0	0

CLEVELAND 4, BOSTON 2

Sox in grave danger

INDIANS SCORE SEVEN IN FIFTH TO TAKE 3-1 SERIES LEAD

By Michael Silverman
BOSTON HERALD
October 17, 2007

CLEVELAND — Even though last night was not a do-or-die proposition for the Red Sox, it sure felt as though the Grim Reaper already was setting up shop in the visitors clubhouse at Jacobs Field.

By tomorrow night, he could be hosting an elimination party.

The Red Sox lost Game 4 of the American League Championship Series, 7-3, in abrupt fashion, with the Indians turning a scoreless game into a seven-run lead in the fifth inning.

With the win, Cleveland carries a commanding 3-1 series lead into Game 5. An off day today will allow plenty of time for Red Sox second-guessers and plain-old fans to gather themselves for tomorrow night's first of what could be as many as three elimination games.

Josh Beckett, the Red Sox ace who many thought should have started last night on short rest, will go in Game 5. C.C. Sabathia will start for the Indians.

"Hopefully the day off will be the day that good karma comes our way," third baseman Mike Lowell said. "I don't think of it as three games in a row we have to win — we just have to focus on winning two days from now."

The Indians' 35-minute fifth drove Sox starter Tim Wakefield out of the game.

The Sox made it a semi-respectable ballgame in the sixth by stroking three solo home runs in a row. Kevin Youkilis, David Ortiz and Manny Ramirez connected in consecutive order. The surge stopped then and there, however, as the

Manny Ramirez gestures to the crowd as he rounds first base after homering in the sixth inning.
(John Wilcox/Boston Herald)

ALCS GAME 4

CLEVELAND 7, BOSTON 3

Center fielder Coco Crisp checks his glove after Casey Blake's fifth-inning RBI single falls in for a hit. Cleveland scored all seven of its runs in the fifth. *(Matthew West/Boston Herald)*

Indians bullpen reverted to its unstoppable form, allowing only one hit to the next dozen batters.

Wakefield held the Indians hitless through the first three innings. After allowing Cleveland its first hit, a two-out double, in the fourth inning, everything fell apart for the knuckleballer in the fifth.

"It's very stunning – you work and you prepare and you do everything you're supposed to do," Wakefield said. "I felt fine, I felt like the ball was moving good."

Like most playoff games, there were funky moments. None of those went the Red Sox' way.

In the Indians fifth, after Casey Blake led off with a home run, Wakefield faced a first-and-third situation with one out. Asdrubal Cabrera hit a foul ball behind first baseman Kevin Youkilis, who, while backpedaling, bobbled it before second baseman Dustin Pedroia got a hand in as well. The ball fell in for no play. With another chance, Cabrera lined a shot up the middle that Wakefield tried to catch, but the ball rolled off his glove and Cabrera had an RBI infield single.

"If I catch it, it's a double play. If I let it go, it's a double play," Wakefield said. "It just nicked the end of my glove."

Said Pedroia: "A lot of things went on that just didn't go our way tonight."

Manny Delcarmen relieved Wakefield and immediately gave up a three-run home run to Jhonny Peralta. When Blake's spot in the order came

ALCS GAME 4

back around in the inning, he completed the scoring with an RBI single.

Indians starter Paul Byrd worked five-plus innings. He departed after serving up the Youkilis and Ortiz home runs. Jensen Lewis came on to allow the Ramirez blast, then settled in through the seventh. Rafael Betancourt worked the eighth and ninth.

"The best thing for us is if we can win (Game 5) and go back home — if we play in front of our fans, it will be huge for us," Youkilis said. "We want to get home. We want to play at home. We feel that we're at our best when we're at home and our fans are behind us. We've got to go out there (tomorrow night) and fight our way back home."

CLEVELAND 7, BOSTON 3 • OCTOBER 16, 2007

	1	2	3	4	5	6	7	8	9		R	H	E
Boston	0	0	0	0	0	3	0	0	0		3	8	1
Cleveland	0	0	0	0	7	0	0	0	X		7	9	0

Boston	AB	R	H	RBI	BB	SO
Pedroia, 2B	4	0	1	0	0	0
Youkilis, 1B	4	1	2	1	0	0
Ortiz, DH	4	1	1	1	0	1
Ramirez, LF	4	1	2	1	0	0
Lowell, 3B	4	0	0	0	0	0
Drew, RF	4	0	1	0	0	1
Crisp, CF	4	0	0	0	0	1
Mirabelli, C	2	0	0	0	0	1
Varitek, C	1	0	1	0	0	0
Lugo, SS	3	0	0	0	0	0
Totals	**34**	**3**	**8**	**3**	**0**	**4**

BATTING
HR: Youkilis (1, 6th inning off Byrd, 0 on, 0 out), Ortiz (1, 6th inning off Byrd, 0 on, 0 out), Ramirez (2, 6th inning off Lewis, 0 on, 0 out).
Team LOB: 4.

FIELDING
E: Youkilis (1, pickoff).

PITCHING

Boston	IP	H	R	ER	BB	SO	HR
Wakefield (L, 0-1)	4.2	5	5	5	2	7	1
Delcarmen	0.1	3	2	2	1	1	1
Lester	3.0	1	0	0	1	4	0

Cleveland	AB	R	H	RBI	BB	SO
Sizemore, CF	3	1	0	0	2	0
Cabrera, 2B	5	1	1	1	0	2
Hafner, DH	4	0	0	0	0	4
Martinez, 1B	4	1	1	1	0	0
Peralta, SS	4	1	2	3	0	1
Lofton, LF	4	1	1	0	0	1
Blake, 3B	4	1	2	2	0	1
Gutierrez, RF	2	1	1	0	2	1
Shoppach, C	3	0	1	0	0	2
Totals	33	7	9	7	4	12

BATTING
2B: Peralta (2, Wakefield).
HR: Blake (1, 5th inning off Wakefield, 0 on, 0 out), Peralta (2, 5th inning off Delcarmen, 2 on, 2 out).
Team LOB: 7.

BASERUNNING
SB: Lofton (1, 2nd base off Delcarmen/Mirabelli), Sizemore (1, 2nd base off Wakefield/Mirabelli).

FIELDING
DP: (Peralta-Cabrera-Martinez).

PITCHING

Cleveland	IP	H	R	ER	BB	SO	HR
Byrd (W, 1-0)	5.0	6	2	2	0	4	2
Lewis	2.0	2	1	1	0	0	1
Betancourt	2.0	0	0	0	0	0	0

CLEVELAND 7, BOSTON 3

Masterpiece sends series back to Hub

BECKETT TO THE RESCUE

By Michael Silverman
BOSTON HERALD
October 19, 2007

CLEVELAND — The Red Sox season has not been canceled due to poor play after all.

"Saturday Night Live" will be beamed from Fenway Park tomorrow.

Starring the Red Sox and with a special guest-host appearance by Curt Schilling, Game 6 of the ALCS was brought home by a spectacular performance from Josh Beckett in a do-or-die Game 5 last night against the Indians.

With Beckett doing everything right — 11 strikeouts, just one walk and five strikeouts — and the offense looking more balanced, the Red Sox flew home, leaving behind a 7-1 victory for the citizens of Cleveland to chew on for a day before they tune in at 8:23 tomorrow night for some must-see TV.

"We're excited to get back to Boston. It's going to be a great flight — better than if we would have went down losing," said Beckett, 3-0 with a 1.17 ERA after three postseason starts. "This is not where we want to be, but obviously we're inching closer to where we want to be. Kind of the motto in the clubhouse right now is, 'It's better to die on your feet than live on your knees.' "

Manny Ramirez, who a day earlier raised some hackles for daring to say that the world would not end if the Red Sox lost, offered a makeup quote for mass consumption.

Looking down at his purple tie as he sat on the couch in the clubhouse, Ramirez said, "I'm trying to take this tie to Colorado."

Red Sox starter Josh Beckett throws to first after fielding a Ryan Garko grounder in the fourth inning.
(Matthew West/Boston Herald)

ALCS GAME 5

BOSTON 7, CLEVELAND 1

Red Sox third baseman Mike Lowell and Indians first base coach Luis Rivera restrained Kenny Lofton as he went after Red Sox starter Josh Beckett, not pictured, after Lofton flew out to left in the fifth inning. *(Matthew West/Boston Herald)*

If Ramirez and the rest of the Red Sox offense can dismantle tomorrow night's Indians starter, Fausto Carmona, as they did in Game 2 — and as they did to C.C. Sabathia (six innings, 10 hits, four runs) last night — it will only make Schilling's job easier.

Kevin Youkilis was the offensive star of the evening, knocking in three runs with a solo home run in the first, an RBI triple in the seventh and a bases-loaded walk in the eighth. With David Ortiz knocking in two runs on a pair of sacrifice flies, Ramirez driving in the go-ahead run with an RBI single that the Red Sox lobbied to be a home run (the umpires got it right) and Dustin Pedroia getting

going with a 2-for-4 effort with a walk and a run, the offense bounced back.

There were a few moments early in the game where the Sox could not drive in a run with runners in scoring position, but by the seventh and eighth innings, everything clicked.

"We really did a good job of getting runners on base early, but we didn't do a whole lot with it. But we stayed at it and stayed at it and finally cashed in — we had good at-bats," said manager Terry Francona.

The game had its moments of high and low drama. At the forefront was a benches-clearing episode in the fifth, when Beckett and Kenny Lofton

ALCS GAME 5

yelled some harsh sentiments at each other. Beckett, saying there was some history between him and Lofton, was apparently upset that Lofton had laid down his bat after what he thought was ball four. On the next pitch, Lofton flied out. Beckett yelled at Lofton, who yelled back and then began walking toward Beckett.

A scrum ensued, but no punches were thrown.

The stakes in tomorrow night's battle will be just as high as they were last night. The Red Sox are still one loss away from the end of the season, one win away from forcing a Game 7.

"We're just trying to play hard on the field and leave everything out there, and whatever happens, happens," said Ramirez. "I've got a lot of confidence in this team — we play hard every day."

By playing hard last night, the Red Sox lived to see another day. They feel they're where they need to be.

"There's no pressure here," said Ramirez. "We've got confidence."

BOSTON 7, CLEVELAND 1 • OCTOBER 18, 2007

	1	2	3	4	5	6	7	8	9		R	H	E
Boston	1	0	1	0	0	0	2	3	0		7	12	1
Cleveland	1	0	0	0	0	0	0	0	0		1	6	1

Boston	AB	R	H	RBI	BB	SO
Pedroia, 2B	4	1	2	0	1	0
Youkilis, 1B	4	2	2	3	1	0
Ortiz, DH	2	1	1	2	1	1
Ramirez, LF	4	0	2	1	1	2
Ellsbury, LF	0	0	0	0	0	0
Lowell, 3B	4	0	1	0	0	1
Kielty, RF	3	0	1	0	0	1
Drew, RF	1	1	1	0	1	0
Varitek, C	4	0	1	0	0	0
Crisp, CF	5	1	0	0	0	2
Lugo, SS	4	1	1	0	0	1
Totals	35	7	12	6	5	8

BATTING
2B: Ramirez (1, Sabathia), Pedroia (1, Sabathia), Drew (1, Mastny).
3B: Youkilis (1, Sabathia).
HR: Youkilis (2, 1st inning off Sabathia, 0 on, 1 out).
Team LOB: 10.

FIELDING
E: Beckett (1, fielding).
DP: (Lugo-Youkilis).

PITCHING

Boston	IP	H	R	ER	BB	SO	HR
Beckett (W, 2-0)	8.0	5	1	1	1	11	0
Papelbon	1.0	1	0	0	1	1	0

Cleveland	AB	R	H	RBI	BB	SO
Sizemore, CF	4	1	2	0	0	1
Cabrera, 2B	4	0	1	0	0	2
Hafner, DH	4	0	0	0	0	2
Martinez, C	4	0	1	0	0	1
Garko, 1B	4	0	1	0	0	2
Peralta, SS	4	0	0	0	0	1
Lofton, LF	3	0	0	0	1	0
Gutierrez, RF	3	0	0	0	1	1
Blake, 3B	3	0	1	0	0	2
Totals	33	1	6	0	2	12

BATTING
2B: Sizemore (2, Beckett), Garko (1, Papelbon).
Team LOB: 7.

FIELDING
E: Perez (1, throw).
PB: Martinez (1).
Outfield assists: Gutierrez (Ramirez at home).
DP: 2 (Sabathia-Peralta-Garko, Peralta-Garko).

PITCHING

Cleveland	IP	H	R	ER	BB	SO	HR
Sabathia (L, 0-2)	6.0	10	4	4	2	6	1
Betancourt	1.0	0	0	0	0	1	0
Perez	0.1	1	3	1	1	0	0
Mastny	1.2	1	0	0	2	1	0

BOSTON 7, CLEVELAND 1

For Sox, victory just how they drew it up

BLOWOUT SETS UP GAME 7

By Jeff Horrigan
BOSTON HERALD
October 21, 2007

The Red Sox could not reach the playing field at Fenway Park last night without passing the enlarged quote from Ryan Garko taped to the back of the clubhouse door.

In an Ohio newspaper a couple of days earlier, the Cleveland Indians first baseman had matter-of-factly stated, "The champagne tastes just as good on the road as it does at home."

After getting pounded by the Sox for the second consecutive game to send the American League Championship Series to a seventh and deciding showdown tonight, that taste test may have to be carried out at an airport lounge just before a somber flight back to Cleveland.

Facing elimination for the second consecutive game, the Sox rode the strong pitching of Curt Schilling and clutch hitting of J.D. Drew to even up the ALCS with a 12-2 drubbing that left them one win away from the World Series.

Daisuke Matsuzaka will oppose Cleveland right-hander Jake Westbrook tonight for the pennant.

Schilling, who lasted only 4⅔ innings in Game 2, rediscovered his old form, allowing only two runs on six hits in seven innings, while striking out five batters. The 40-year-old improved to 10-2 lifetime in postseason play, including 4-0 with a 1.37 ERA in five starts when his team could have been eliminated. An impending free agent, he faced the possibility that he may have pitched his last game at Fenway for the Sox.

"God gave me a chance to play professional baseball, which is a gift beyond anything you'd ever dreamed of, but to

Starter Curt Schilling mulls things over in the dugout prior to Game 6. Schilling pitched seven strong innings as the Red Sox won to force a Game 7. *(Matthew West/Boston Herald)*

ALCS GAME 6

BOSTON 12, CLEVELAND 2

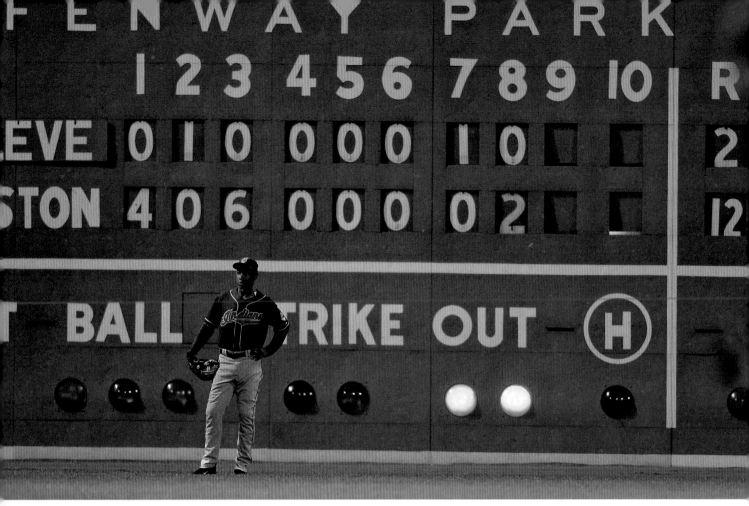

Cleveland left fielder Kenny Lofton stands dejected beneath the green monster scoreboard showing what became the game's final score. *(Matthew West/Boston Herald)*

play in this environment, in this stadium, in front of these people, I would argue that you'll never hear home-field advantage being pooh-poohed again in this city," Schilling said.

After a disappointing first season in Boston, Drew (3-for-5, five RBI) finally pulled Fenway fans over to his side by slamming a tone-setting, first-inning grand slam off Fausto Carmona. The Sox hammered Carmona for seven runs on six hits and four walks in two-plus innings to make this one a laugher early.

"I didn't have the year I would have liked to have, but I feel like I had a good September and started getting things turned around," Drew said.

Cleveland came into the series with a distinct swagger, knowing that it could rely on the seemingly unparalleled, 1-2 pitching punch provided by C.C. Sabathia and Carmona. The Sox, however, handled them with ease, saddling them with a 0-3 record and 12.67 ERA in their four starts. The duo allowed 23 earned runs on 27 hits and 16 walks in only 16⅓ innings.

Carmona, who went 19-8 during the regular season, struggled when the Sox laid off his hard sinker, which often ends up out of the strike zone, and forced him to put the ball over the plate. They parlayed that discerning eye into 11 earned runs on 10 hits and nine walks over six combined innings in this series.

ALCS GAME 6

Dustin Pedroia and Kevin Youkilis opened the first inning with successive infield singles before David Ortiz drew a walk to load the bases with no outs. Carmona struck out Manny Ramirez and got Mike Lowell on a shallow fly ball to come within an out of marooning three runners, but he left a 97 mph, knee-high fastball over the plate to Drew, who crushed it with the speed, distance and straightness of a well-struck 3-wood, sending it over the center field wall for the sixth grand slam in ALCS history.

Victor Martinez cut the lead to 4-1 by leading off the second with a homer blasted over Pesky's Pole, but Schilling held it there. The Sox put the game away with a six-run third inning, sending 11 batters to the plate. Julio Lugo delivered a two-run double and Drew, Youkilis and Jacoby Ellsbury hit RBI singles.

BOSTON 12, CLEVELAND 2 • OCTOBER 20, 2007

	1	2	3	4	5	6	7	8	9	R	H	E
Cleveland	0	1	0	0	0	0	1	0	0	2	6	2
Boston	4	0	6	0	0	0	0	2	X	12	13	0

Cleveland	AB	R	H	RBI	BB	SO
Sizemore, CF	4	0	0	0	0	0
Cabrera, 2B	4	0	0	0	0	0
Hafner, DH	4	0	0	0	0	2
Martinez, C	4	1	2	1	0	1
Garko, 1B	4	1	1	0	0	1
Peralta, SS	2	0	0	1	0	1
Lofton, LF	3	0	0	0	0	0
Nixon, RF	3	0	2	0	0	0
Blake, 3B	3	0	1	0	0	0
Totals	**31**	**2**	**6**	**2**	**0**	**5**

BATTING
3B: Garko (1, Schilling).
HR: Martinez (1, 2nd inning off Schilling, 0 on, 0 out).
Team LOB: 3.

FIELDING
E: Cabrera (1, throw).
Outfield assists: Lofton (Pedroia at home).
DP: (Peralta-Garko).

PITCHING

Cleveland	IP	H	R	ER	BB	SO	HR
Carmona (L, 0-1)	2.0	6	7	7	4	2	1
Perez	0.1	3	3	2	1	0	0
Laffey	4.2	1	0	0	1	3	0
Borowski	1.0	3	2	2	2	0	0

Boston	AB	R	H	RBI	BB	SO
Pedroia, 2B	4	2	2	0	1	0
Youkilis, 1B	4	2	3	1	1	0
Ortiz, DH	4	1	1	0	1	1
1-Hinske, PR-DH	0	1	0	0	0	0
Ramirez, LF	2	1	0	1	2	1
Crisp, CF	0	0	0	0	0	0
Lowell, 3B	4	1	2	1	1	0
Drew, RF	5	2	3	5	0	1
Varitek, C	3	0	0	0	2	0
Ellsbury, CF-LF	5	1	1	1	0	1
Lugo, SS	4	1	1	2	0	1
Cora, SS	0	0	0	0	0	0
Totals	35	12	13	11	8	5

1-Ran for Ortiz in the 8th.

BATTING
2B: Pedroia (2, Carmona), Lugo (2, Perez), Ortiz (3, Borowski).
HR: Drew (1, 1st inning off Carmona, 3 on, 2 out).
Team LOB: 8.

FIELDING
DP: (Pedroia-Lugo-Youkilis).

PITCHING

Boston	IP	H	R	ER	BB	SO	HR
Schilling (W, 1-0)	7.0	6	2	2	0	5	1
Lopez	1.0	0	0	0	0	0	0
Gagne	1.0	0	0	0	0	0	0

BOSTON 12, CLEVELAND 2

The comeback kings

WIN PUTS SOX BACK IN SERIES

By Jeff Horrigan
BOSTON HERALD
October 22, 2007

It's probably safe to assume that there are more than a few lumps in the throats around the base of the Rocky Mountains today, considering how the Red Sox reacted to being backed into a corner by the Cleveland Indians in the American League Championship Series.

Down 3-1 in the best-of-seven format, the Sox reacted like vicious attack dogs, mauling the Indians by a combined score of 30-5 in the final three games, culminated by an 11-2 thumping last night that wrapped up the pennant and sent them back to the World Series for the second time in four years.

The Sox, who became the 11th team to rally from a 3-1 deficit and win a postseason series, humiliated the Indians in every sense to earn the right to host the Colorado Rockies in Game 1 on Wednesday. The National League champs enter their first Fall Classic having won 21 of their last 22 games.

"When we had our backs to the wall, we didn't let our guards down and just take the beating," said Coco Crisp, whose dramatic catch against the wall in center field ended the clincher. "We fought back and fought back hard."

Kevin Youkilis, who established an ALCS record with a .500 batting average, reminded teammates afterward of the bulletin-board fodder that Cleveland first baseman Ryan Garko had provided.

"I'll tell you what: The champagne tastes better at home," he shouted as he sprayed teammates, referring to Garko's postgame comments last Thursday, when he said that the Indians' champagne would taste just as good in Boston.

Red Sox closer Jonathan Papelbon and catcher Jason Varitek celebrate after Boston's victory over Cleveland in Game 7 of the American League Championship Series.
(Stuart Cahill/Boston Herald)

ALCS GAME 7

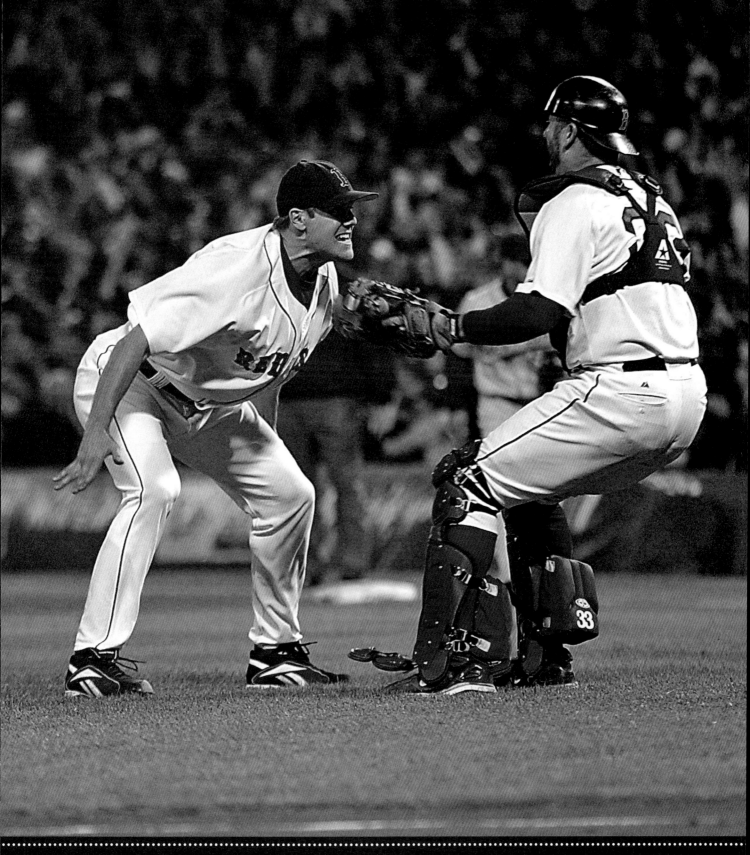

BOSTON 11, CLEVELAND 2

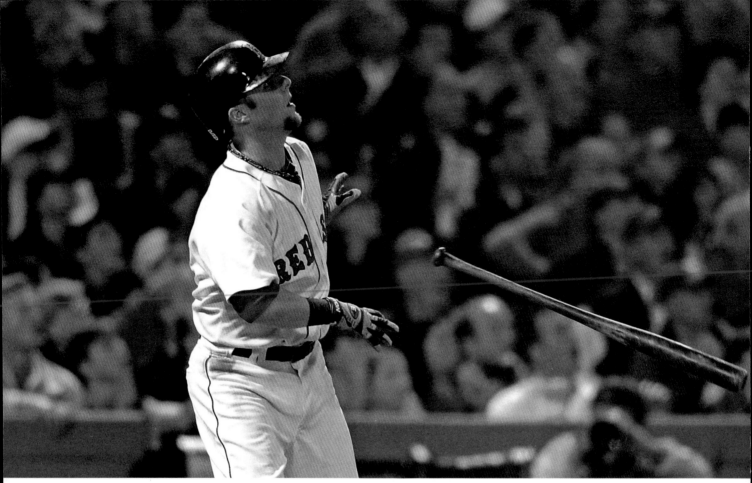

Second baseman Dustin Pedroia hits a two-run homer in the seventh inning to give the Red Sox a 5-2 lead. *(Matthew West/Boston Herald)*

The Sox jumped out to a 3-0 lead with individual runs in each of the first three innings, saw that advantage cut to one in the fifth and then broke things open with a combined eight runs in the seventh and eighth.

After lasting only four innings in each of his first two postseason starts, Daisuke Matsuzaka stuck around for five this time before departing with a 3-2 lead. He gave up six hits, struck out three and walked none but saw a marked drop-off in effectiveness in his final two frames, when the Indians scored single runs.

Hideki Okajima followed with two scoreless innings of relief before Jonathan Papelbon wrapped up his first career two-inning save.

"We just kept putting good at-bats together when we needed to, and everything seemed to click at the same time," Pedroia said. "That's how we turned it around."

The early 3-0 lead potentially could have been much larger had the Sox not let Cleveland starter Jake Westbrook off the hook by bouncing into deflating double plays in three of the first four frames.

Singles by Pedroia, Youkilis and Manny Ramirez (RBI) gave them a 1-0 lead in the first, before Game 6 hero J.D. Drew bounced into an inning-ending DP.

Jason Varitek's leadoff double off the Green Monster and Jacoby Ellsbury's ensuing hit put two men on base with no outs in the second, but Julio Lugo's run-scoring DP grounder did away with the big-inning potential.

Youkilis led off the third with a double to left and scored on Mike Lowell's sacrifice fly, but an inning

ALCS GAME 7

later, a two-on, one-out scenario was wasted when Pedroia grounded into another inning-ending DP.

From there, Westbrook settled down, allowing three runs on nine hits and striking out five before leaving after the sixth.

Matsuzaka, meanwhile, had all of his pitches working early, including a blazing, mid-90s fastball. He retired 10 of the first 11 batters before Cleveland broke through in the fourth on doubles by Travis Hafner and Garko.

He barely made it through the fifth, when the Indians opened the inning with three successive singles but managed to score only one run on Grady Sizemore's sacrifice fly. Ramirez played a vital role by throwing out Kenny Lofton attempting to stretch a leadoff single off the left field scoreboard into a double.

The Sox broke open the close game in the seventh on Pedroia's two-run homer off reliever Rafael Betancourt. The rookie second baseman then allowed the partying to begin by slamming a three-run, bases-loaded double in a six-run eighth. Youkilis followed with a two-run blast off reliever Jensen Lewis.

That capped the Sox' seventh straight win in an ALCS elimination game.

BOSTON 11, CLEVELAND 2 • OCTOBER 21, 2007

	1	2	3	4	5	6	7	8	9	R	H	E
Cleveland	0	0	0	1	1	0	0	0	0	2	10	1
Boston	1	1	0	0	0	2	6	1	X	11	15	1

Cleveland	AB	R	H	RBI	BB	SO
Sizemore, CF	3	0	1	1	0	1
Cabrera, 2B	4	0	1	0	0	1
Hafner, DH	4	1	1	0	0	2
Martinez, C	4	0	0	0	0	0
Garko, 1B	4	0	1	1	0	0
Peralta, SS	4	0	1	0	0	0
Lofton, LF	4	0	1	0	0	0
Gutierrez, RF	4	1	2	0	0	0
Blake, 3B	4	0	2	0	0	0
Totals	35	2	10	2	0	4

BATTING
2B: Hafner (1, Matsuzaka), Garko (2, Matsuzaka).
Team LOB: 7.

FIELDING
E: Blake (1, fielding).
DP: 3 (Peralta-Cabrera-Garko 2, Cabrera-Garko).

PITCHING
Cleveland	IP	H	R	ER	BB	SO	HR
Westbrook (L, 1-1)	6.0	9	3	3	1	5	0
Betancourt	1.2	5	7	6	1	1	1
Lewis	0.1	1	1	1	0	1	1

Boston	AB	R	H	RBI	BB	SO
Pedroia, 2B	5	3	3	5	0	0
Youkilis, 1B	5	2	3	2	0	1
Ortiz, DH	5	0	0	0	0	2
Ramirez, LF	3	0	1	1	1	1
Crisp, CF	0	0	0	0	0	0
Lowell, 3B	3	1	2	1	0	1
Drew, RF	4	1	1	1	0	0
Varitek, C	4	2	3	0	0	1
Ellsbury, CF-LF	3	2	1	0	1	0
Lugo, SS	3	0	1	0	0	1
Totals	35	11	15	10	2	7

BATTING
2B: Varitek 2 (3, Westbrook, Betancourt), Youkilis (1, Westbrook), Lowell (2, Betancourt), Pedroia (3, Betancourt).
HR: Pedroia (1, 7th inning off Betancourt, 1 on, 1 out), Youkilis (3, 8th inning off Lewis, 1 on, 2 out).
Team LOB: 4.

FIELDING
E: Lugo (1, fielding).
Outfield assists: Ramirez (Lofton at 2nd base).
DP: (Lowell-Pedroia-Youkilis).

PITCHING
Boston	IP	H	R	ER	BB	SO	HR
Matsuzaka (W, 1-1)	5.0	6	2	2	0	3	0
Okajima (H, 1)	2.0	3	0	0	0	0	0
Papelbon (S, 1)	2.0	1	0	0	0	1	0

BOSTON 11, CLEVELAND 2

(Stuart Cahill/Boston Herald)

WORLD SERIES

PITCHER
JOSH BECKETT
THIS REBEL HAS A CAUSE

By Tony Massarotti
BOSTON HERALD
October 24, 2007

What we have here, by all accounts, is a gunslingin, brash-talkin, tall-walkin cowboy, right down to every last detail.

In the baseball sense, Josh Beckett is part Roger Clemens, part Pedro Martinez and part Curt Schilling, the aces who have preceded him in the Red Sox line of kings.

In the Hollywood sense, Beckett is more like John McClane, the renegade New York City police detective in the Die Hard series who was reckless, fearless and arrogant enough to believe he could make a difference.

Yippee ki-yay (fill in the blank)!

"He can be a bit of an antiestablishment guy from time to time, but I don't think theres anything wrong with that – a contrarian, I guess," Red Sox general manager Theo Epstein said of Beckett. "If you tell him east, he'll say west even if he knows its east."

What Beckett knows now, like everyone, is that the world is watching, even if he will not necessarily admit it. Speaking at Fenway Park yesterday in anticipation of his World Series Game 1 start against the Colorado Rockies tonight, Beckett continued to talk with both disdain and contempt. Ask Beckett what he is doing differently to excel on this, baseballs grandest stage, and he all but delivers the answer with a sneer.

Nothing.

In the last 70 years, among all major league pitchers with at least 50 career postseason innings, Beckett's 1.78 ERA ranks third, behind only Mariano Rivera (0.77) and Sandy Koufax (0.95). In Rivera's case, he was a closer who never had to face the same hitters three or four times in a game; as for Koufax, he pitched in an era that existed before the advent of the designated hitter.

BIG-GAME HUNTER

Long before he won 20 games this season, long before he even arrived in Boston with an air that suggested he was unimpressed by it all, Beckett had the swagger of a 300-game winner.

He was often referred to as cocky, said Red Sox principal owner John Henry, who owned the Marlins when they chose Beckett with the No. 2 overall selection in the 1999 amateur draft. Dave Dombrowski (then the Marlins general manager) saw that as a vital ingredient because he thought that translated into confidence. We did quite a bit of studying (on Beckett).

Taking a high school pitcher with the second pick in the draft back then, that was a lot of money.

Of course, Beckett's ascension drew predictable attention, culminating with his performance against the New York Yankees in the decisive Game 6 of the 2003 World Series. Much like the current Rockies, the 2003 Marlins were a young, talented team that matured greatly through the season, resulting in a spirited, second-half run that brought them to the postseason.

What the Marlins lacked, many believed before the start of the playoffs, was experience, particularly on the pitching staff. But in his first postseason, after a regular season during which he went a mere 9-8, Beckett pitched in six games, posting a 2.11 ERA and averaging 9.7 strikeouts per nine innings while authoring a pair of complete-game shutouts.

At the time, Beckett was just 23. Still, Henry had long since recognized what Dombrowski saw in Beckett and what 2003 Marlins manager Jack McKeon also would identify: his ability to intensify his focus at those moments that called for it.

"I went to see his first game at Double A (in 2001), and the jump to Double A can be a tough jump," Henry said. "I think we counted something like 37 or 47 pitches before a batter even made contact. That confidence is a result of just knowing how good your stuff is."

Said McKeon when asked about Beckett's nature: "He's a fearless guy and he loves the big stage, and that's the kind of guy you want. You like to see that in a guy. You don't want to take that away from him."

Especially at times like these.

NO BACKING DOWN

Had Beckett done to the Red Sox what he did to the Cleveland Indians, Red Sox followers might regard him as, well, a thug.

The Most Valuable Player of the American League Championship Series did not merely shut down the Indians; in pivotal Game 5, he also shouted at left fielder Kenny Lofton for prematurely walking toward first base on a close 3-0 pitch called a strike.

In that way, Beckett is very much like Martinez, who was known to drill a hitter (or two) for stepping out of the batters box during his delivery.

The message?

This is my game. How dare you.

"I think there is some volatility there," Henry admitted. "A lot of players don't show it, but it's there. With some players, in the heat of competition, they can erupt. We've seen it with David (Ortiz) and we've even seen it with Manny (Ramirez). I think that's all it is. The adrenaline's flowing."

Whatever the explanation, Beckett's on-field behavior has been well documented. Last year, during his inaugural spring training with the Red Sox, Beckett chastised Philadelphia Phillies slugger Ryan Howard for watching a home run. The Lofton incident only offered further evidence that the on-field Beckett is something of a bully, like his idol, the accomplished Roger Clemens.

Through it all, he has established his place as

(Matthew West/Boston Herald)

the Sox best big-game pitcher since, well, Schilling.

"They're different pitchers now, though," Red Sox manager Terry Francona said yesterday. "You see a guy that's been doing it for a long time (in Schilling) and knows how to do it, doesn't quite throw like he used to, but still knows how to pitch and how to win."

As for Beckett?

"You see the other guy that's starting to come into his own and make a name for himself," Francona said. "He's younger, starting to mature, and were reaping the benefits of that because he's maturing right in front of our eyes. Seems like every game he wants to make more of a name for himself."

History repeats

ROUT PARALLELS '04 SWEEP

By Jeff Horrigan
BOSTON HERALD
October 25, 2007

With bespectacled men in tri-cornered hats still dotting the Freedom Trail with tour groups, John F. Kennedy still as revered as he was after his first election victory, and historical markers more prevalent than road signs, it's safe to say folks in this area enjoy living in the past.

Around Fenway Park these days, however, most of the nostalgia has to do with events from three years ago. Three nights after another miraculous escape in the American League Championship Series, the Red Sox humiliated the Colorado Rockies, 13-1, last night with an offensive barrage that even surpassed the 11-run outburst in Game 1 of their 2004 sweep of the St. Louis Cardinals.

The Sox reached out for the Rockies' collective throat with a three-run first inning, keyed by Dustin Pedroia's leadoff home run. They never relinquished their grip en route to the second-largest margin in a Fall Classic game, and they ended a Rockies run in which Colorado had won 10 straight and 21-of-22.

"That's not the way we drew it up," Rockies manager Clint Hurdle said.

ALCS MVP Josh Beckett again was dominant, improving to 4-0 with a 1.20 ERA in four starts this postseason. He allowed one run on six hits with nine strikeouts in seven innings.

"He's been huge for us," Sox manager Terry Francona said. "To win, you have to have guys like that. Every time we've gone to him, he's given us a great outing, and we certainly hope that continues."

As the rain picked up in the fourth inning, so did Josh Beckett's performance. The Red Sox starter picked up his sixth and seventh strikeouts in the fourth frame.
(Matthew West/Boston Herald)

WORLD SERIES GAME 1

BOSTON 13, COLORADO 1

Colorado starter Jeff Francis didn't come close to duplicating his June 14 start, in which he beat Beckett, 7-1, at Fenway. The lefty was hammered for six runs on 10 hits in four innings before reliever Franklin Morales surrendered seven runs in a game-breaking fifth.

The Sox collected eight doubles, tying a World Series record held by the 1906 Chicago White Sox and 1925 Pittsburgh Pirates.

One of the fears for the Rockies was that their eight-day break after the NLCS would disrupt their timing at the plate, and they did nothing to dispel that notion. Beckett struck out the first four batters he faced, joining Mort Cooper (five in 1943) and Sandy Koufax (five in 1963) as the only pitchers to achieve the feat in the World Series.

"I think I executed just enough pitches to survive," Beckett said with a straight face.

The Sox, who had only two days off after completing the ALCS, were sharp from the start. Pedroia delivered an immediate, stunning blow to the Rockies by jumping on Francis' second pitch of the game and lining it just over the Green Monster for the rookie's second postseason homer. It also was the 11th first-inning leadoff homer in World Series history and the first since the Sox' Johnny Damon opened Game 4 of the 2004 sweep of St. Louis.

The Sox were far from done. After batting an eye-popping .500 (14-for-28) in the ALCS, Kevin Youkilis kept up his torrid run by following with a double lined to the gap in right-center. Manny Ramirez knocked him in two batters later with a single to left, giving the cleanup hitter 63 career post-

Kevin Youkilis beats the throw home to score on a David Ortiz double in the second inning. *(Matthew West/Boston Herald)*

WORLD SERIES GAME 1

BOSTON 13, COLORADO 1

WORLD SERIES GAME 1

season RBI, tied with David Justice for second all-time.

Jason Varitek's two-out single kept the rally alive, and the revived J.D. Drew, followed with a double to the right field corner that knocked in Ramirez with the third Sox run.

Jason Varitek races for home as Colorado third base-man Garrett Atkins tries to make the play on a Julio Lugo grounder. Varitek was 2-4 with a run scored. *(Nancy Lane/Boston Herald)*

The Rockies got a run in the second, but the Sox responded with one in the bottom half on David Ortiz' RBI double before tacking on two more in the fourth on Varitek's two-run double. They broke things open in the fifth, thanks in part to Ryan Speier's three-consecutive bases-loaded walks.

"We definitely had a lot of momentum going," said Youkilis, who was 2-for-5 with three runs scored. "Those last three games against the Indians, we were rolling on all cylinders. Guys were feeling a little more comfortable at the plate."

BOSTON 13, COLORADO 1 • OCTOBER 24, 2007

	1	2	3	4	5	6	7	8	9	R	H	E
Colorado	0	1	0	0	0	0	0	0	0	1	6	0
Boston	3	1	0	2	7	0	0	0	X	13	17	0

Colorado	AB	R	H	RBI	BB	SO
Taveras, CF	4	0	0	0	0	2
Matsui, 2B	4	0	1	0	0	1
Holliday, LF	4	0	0	0	0	2
Helton, 1B	4	0	2	0	0	1
Atkins, 3B	4	1	1	0	0	1
Hawpe, RF	4	0	0	0	0	4
Tulowitzki, SS	3	0	2	1	0	0
Torrealba, C	3	0	0	0	0	1
Spilborghs, DH	2	0	0	0	1	0
Totals	**32**	**1**	**6**	**1**	**1**	**12**

BATTING
2B: Atkins (1, Beckett), Tulowitzki 2 (2, Beckett, Beckett), Helton (1, Beckett).
Team LOB: 5.

PITCHING

Colorado	IP	H	R	ER	BB	SO	HR
Francis (L, 0-1)	4.0	10	6	6	3	3	1
Morales	0.2	6	7	7	1	0	0
Speier	0.0	0	0	0	3	0	0
Herges	1.1	0	0	0	1	1	0
Affeldt	1.0	1	0	0	0	0	0
Hawkins	1.0	0	0	0	0	2	0

Boston	AB	R	H	RBI	BB	SO
Pedroia, 2B	5	1	1	2	1	0
Youkilis, 1B	5	3	2	1	1	1
Ortiz, DH	5	2	3	2	0	0
a-Hinske, PH-DH	1	0	0	0	0	1
Ramirez, LF	4	3	3	2	1	0
Crisp, CF	1	0	0	0	0	0
Lowell, 3B	3	1	1	0	2	0
Varitek, C	4	1	2	2	1	2
Drew, RF	5	1	2	2	0	1
Lugo, SS	4	0	3	1	1	0
Cora, SS	0	0	0	0	0	0
Ellsbury, CF-LF	4	1	0	1	1	1
Totals	**41**	**13**	**17**	**13**	**8**	**6**

a-Struck out for Ortiz in the 8th.

BATTING
2B: Youkilis 2 (2, Francis, Morales), Drew (1, Francis), Ortiz 2 (2, Francis, Morales), Ramirez (1, Francis), Varitek (1, Francis), Lowell (1, Morales).
HR: Pedroia (1, 1st inning off Francis, 0 on, 0 out).
Team LOB: 12.

FIELDING
DP: (Pedroia-Lugo-Youkilis).

PITCHING

Boston	IP	H	R	ER	BB	SO	HR
Beckett (W, 1-0)	7.0	6	1	1	1	9	0
Timlin	1.0	0	0	0	0	2	0
Gagne	1.0	0	0	0	0	1	0

BOSTON 13, COLORADO 1

Old faithful!

SCHILLING, BULLPEN BRILLIANT IN TENSE WIN

By Jeff Horrigan
BOSTON HERALD
October 26, 2007

If Curt Schilling pitched his final home game at Fenway Park last night, he has only himself to blame.

Of course, neither he nor anyone else in New England will complain about the way he went out if his effort in Game 2 of the World Series was his farewell. Schilling, who will be a free agent after the series, allowed only one run on four hits in 5 1/3solid innings, leading the Red Sox to a 2-1 victory over the Colorado Rockies and a commanding 2-0 lead in the best-of-seven series.

The 40-year-old struck out four batters, walked two and held the Rockies hitless in four at-bats with runners in scoring position to improve to an unparalleled 11-2 with a 2.23 ERA in 19 career postseason starts.

"Whatever happens is going to happen," Schilling said. "I have faith in God that it's going to work out the way it's supposed to work out. They know what I want and they know I want to come back, and we'll deal with that at an appropriate time. We're trying to win a World Series, so it makes it very, very easy not to even think about it."

Relievers Hideki Okajima (2 1/3 shutout innings, four strikeouts) and Jonathan Papelbon (second postseason save) preserved the Sox' first one-run victory of the postseason.

"This was just the Papa-Jima Show tonight," praised Schilling. "That was just phenomenal to watch — Okajima was just absolutely perfect every single pitch."

The Sox, who pounded the Rockies, 13-1, in the series opener on Wednesday, are looking to become the seventh consecutive team with a 2-0 lead to capture the World Series.

Curt Schilling tips his hat to the crowd after leaving in the sixth inning. A free agent after the 2007 season, Schilling may have made his last start in a Red Sox uniform in Game 2. *(Matthew West/Boston Herald)*

WORLD SERIES GAME 2

BOSTON 2, COLORADO 1

WORLD SERIES GAME 2

Rockies left fielder Matt Holliday is picked off by Red Sox closer Jonathan Papelbon in the eighth inning. Kevin Youkilis applies the tag. *(Matt Stone/Boston Herald)*

The Fall Classic will resume tomorrow night at Coors Field in Denver.

"We've done a lot of things that people haven't expected us to do all year," Rockies manager Clint Hurdle said. "We've been down to one strike (away from) going home. Game 3 is now the most important game for us."

Rockies starting pitcher Ubaldo Jimenez lasted only 4 2/3 innings and surrendered two runs on three hits and five walks before a high pitch count (91) sent him to an early exit. The 23-year-old rook-

Hideki Okajima pitches in the sixth inning. *(Nancy Lane/Boston Herald)*

ie received a 1-0 lead in the first inning but paid the price when his command began to wane.

After stranding a pair of walked runners in the third, he issued a one-out base on balls to Mike Lowell in the fourth, which was immediately followed by J.D. Drew's lined single to right field. Jason Varitek then tied it with a sacrifice fly to deep center field.

The Sox, who scored 11 two-out runs on Wednesday, continued the trend in the fifth, allowing them to push across the eventual winning run. Jimenez issued a two-out walk to David Ortiz [stats] before giving up consecutive hits to Manny Ramirez [stats] and Lowell on offspeed pitches. Ramirez bounced a 1-and-2 changeup through the left side,

WORLD SERIES GAME 2

and Lowell followed by lining a 2-and-1 slider down the left field line for a tiebreaking double.

Schilling, who staved off elimination in the ALCS last Saturday by leading the Sox to a 12-2 victory over Cleveland, pitched poorly vs. Colorado during the regular season on June 13 (a 12-2 loss), but that was before he began a shift away from power pitching due to shoulder troubles.

The change in styles, however, did little to prevent him from immediately falling behind last night. He grazed Willy Taveras on the left hand to open the game, and Matt Holliday (4-for-4) followed two bat-

ters with a hard grounder down the third base line that deflected off the glove of the diving Lowell for a base hit. Todd Helton, who came into the game with only one RBI in the postseason, knocked in Taveras with a groundout to first base.

That was the last trouble that Schilling would encounter until the sixth, when he began tightening up in the chilly weather and allowed a one-out single to Holliday, followed by a walk to Helton. Manager Terry Francona called on Okajima, who stranded the runners by getting Garrett Atkins to ground out before striking out Brad Hawpe on three pitches.

Papelbon preserved the lead in the eighth by picking off Holliday at first base following a two-out single.

Jonathan Papelbon reacts after getting the final out of Game 2. *(Nancy Lane/Boston Herald)*

BOSTON 2, COLORADO 1 • OCTOBER 25, 2007

	1	2	3	4	5	6	7	8	9	R	H	E
Colorado	1	0	0	0	0	0	0	0	0	1	5	0
Boston	0	0	0	1	1	0	0	0	X	2	6	1

Colorado	AB	R	H	RBI	BB	SO
Taveras, CF	3	1	0	0	0	1
Matsui, 2B	4	0	0	0	0	2
Holliday, LF	4	0	4	0	0	0
Helton, 1B	3	0	0	1	1	1
Atkins, 3B	4	0	0	0	0	0
Hawpe, RF	4	0	1	0	0	2
Tulowitzki, SS	2	0	0	0	1	1
Torrealba, C	2	0	0	0	0	0
Spilborghs, DH	3	0	0	0	0	3
Totals	29	1	5	1	2	10

BATTING
Team LOB: 5.

BASERUNNING
PO: Holliday (1st base by Papelbon).

PITCHING

Colorado	IP	H	R	ER	BB	SO	HR
Jimenez (L, 0-1)	4.2	3	2	2	5	2	0
Affeldt	0.0	0	0	0	1	0	0
Herges	1.0	1	0	0	1	0	0
Fuentes	2.0	1	0	0	0	1	0
Corpas	0.1	1	0	0	0	0	0

Boston	AB	R	H	RBI	BB	SO
Pedroia, 2B	4	0	1	0	1	0
Youkilis, 1B	3	0	0	0	2	0
Ortiz, DH	3	1	0	0	1	1
Ramirez, LF	4	0	1	0	0	0
Lowell, 3B	3	1	1	1	1	0
Drew, RF	2	0	2	0	1	0
Varitek, C	3	0	0	1	0	2
Ellsbury, CF	3	0	1	0	1	0
Lugo, SS	3	0	0	0	0	0
Totals	28	2	6	2	7	3

BATTING
2B: Lowell (2, Jimenez).
Team LOB: 12.

BASERUNNING
SB: Ellsbury (1, 2nd base off Jimenez/Torrealba).

FIELDING
E: Lowell (1, throw).
DP: (Lugo-Youkilis).
Pickoffs: Papelbon (Holliday at 1st base).

PITCHING

Boston	IP	H	R	ER	BB	SO	HR
Schilling (W, 1-0)	5.1	4	1	1	2	4	0
Okajima (H, 1)	2.1	0	0	0	0	4	0
Papelbon (S, 1)	1.1	1	0	0	0	2	0

BOSTON 2, COLORADO 1

Slice 'N' Dice

SOX A WIN AWAY FROM MAKING MORE HISTORY

By Jeff Horrigan
BOSTON HERALD
October 28, 2007

DENVER — Daisuke Matsuzaka, Jacoby Ellsbury and Dustin Pedroia were in Japan, Oregon and Arizona, respectively, when the Red Sox last won the World Series in 2004, but their unified presence last night in Game 3 of this year's Fall Classic allowed the Sox to move within one victory of another title.

Matsuzaka, who had just finished his sixth season with the Seibu Lions when the Sox won it all in 2004, pitched 5 1/3 strong innings and knocked in two runs with a single in a key six-run third inning, while fellow rookies Ellsbury and Pedroia combined to go 7-for-10 with four runs batted in, four doubles and three runs scored from the top two spots in the batting order in a 10-5 victory at Coors Field.

Ellsbury, who was a junior at Oregon State in '04, went 4-for-5 with three doubles, two RBI and two runs out of the leadoff spot. Pedroia, who was playing in the Arizona Fall League after his first pro season three years ago, went 3-for-5 with a double and two RBI out of the No. 2 hole.

"They're performing like they've been here a long time," said shortstop Julio Lugo (1-for-3, two walks, two runs). "They know they belong here and they're performing like this at a time when we need them."

The victory provided the Sox a commanding, 3-0 series lead and presented Jon Lester, who was battling lymphoma at this time last year, the opportunity to wrap up the franchise's seventh title when he starts Game 4 tonight. No team that has won the first three games of a World Series has failed to capture the title.

Closer Jonathan Papelbon celebrates the last out with catcher Jason Varitek.
(Matt Stone/Boston Herald)

WORLD SERIES GAME 3

BOSTON 10, COLORADO 5

"Let's see what's going to happen (tonight)," said left fielder Manny Ramirez, the only starter not to register a hit (0-for-4, walk). "We don't want to eat the cake before your birthday."

The Sox jumped out to a 6-0 lead but saw the Rockies climb back to within a run by scoring twice in the sixth inning and three more times in the seventh on a Matt Holliday home run off reliever Hideki Okajima. In the eighth, however, the Red Sox responded with a three-run burst highlighted by Ellsbury and Pedroia doubles.

"I just tried to do what got me here and be a lot more aggressive in the strike zone," Ellsbury said. "Fortunately, the balls fell for me."

Jonathan Papelbon recorded the final four outs for the second consecutive game, and in the process registered postseason save No. 3.

Rockies starter Josh Fogg was hammered for six runs on 10 hits and two walks in only 2 2/3 innings. He completely fell apart in the third, when the Sox sent 11 batters to the plate. In the third, Ellsbury became the second player in World Series history to record two doubles in an inning, joining the Arizona Diamondbacks' Matt Williams (Game 6, 2001), and Matsuzaka delivered the crushing blow.

The first five batters reached in the third, including David Ortiz, who followed Ellsbury's leadoff double and Pedroia's bunt single by sending an RBI double to the right field corner. Fogg then issued an intentional walk to Ramirez, a strategy that backfired when Mike Lowell bounced a two-run single up the middle. Ramirez was then thrown out at the plate by Holliday attempting to score on Jason Varitek's one-out single to left field, but the Sox managed to manufacture three more runs. Colorado pitched around Julio Lugo to get to

Dustin Pedroia bunts for a single in the third inning. *(Matthew West/Boston Herald)*

WORLD SERIES GAME 3

BOSTON 10, COLORADO 5

ABOVE: Manny Ramirez is tagged out by Yorvit Torrealba in the third inning of Game 3. *(Stuart Cahill/Boston Herald)*
BELOW: Manny Ramirez pleads his case with home plate umpire Ted Barrett. *(Nancy Lane/Boston Herald)*

Matsuzaka but Fogg made a tactical mistake by throwing a first-pitch curveball that the Sox pitcher poked through the left side of the infield for a two-run single.

Matsuzaka's hit was the first by a Red Sox pitcher in World Series play since Bill Lee's fourth-inning single against Cincinnati's Don Gullett in Game 7 of the 1975 Fall Classic. Ellsbury followed Matsuzaka with another double to the left-center field gap to knock in Lugo with the inning's sixth run.

Matsuzaka cruised through the first four innings before his effectiveness began waning. He stranded a pair of runners in the fifth and was lifted in the sixth after issuing a pair of one-out walks. Brad Hawpe and Yorvit Torrealba greeted reliever Javier Lopez with consecutive RBI singles before Mike Timlin stranded two runners.

Okajima and Manny Delcarmen then preceded Papelbon out of the bullpen.

BOSTON 10, COLORADO 5 • OCTOBER 27, 2007

	1	2	3	4	5	6	7	8	9	R	H	E
Boston	0	0	6	0	0	0	0	3	1	10	15	1
Colorado	0	0	0	0	0	2	3	0	0	5	11	0

Boston	AB	R	H	RBI	BB	SO
Ellsbury, CF-RF	5	2	4	2	0	0
Pedroia, 2B	5	1	3	2	0	0
Papelbon, P	0	0	0	0	0	0
Ortiz, 1B	4	1	1	1	0	2
Youkilis, 1B	1	0	0	0	0	0
Ramirez, LF	4	0	0	0	1	1
Lowell, 3B	5	2	2	2	0	1
Drew, RF	4	0	1	0	0	1
Okajima, P	0	0	0	0	0	0
Delcarmen, P	0	0	0	0	0	0
Cora, 2B	0	0	0	0	0	0
Varitek, C	4	1	1	1	0	1
Lugo, SS	3	2	1	0	2	0
Matsuzaka, P	3	0	1	2	0	1
Lopez, P	0	0	0	0	0	0
Timlin, P	0	0	0	0	0	0
Crisp, CF	1	1	1	0	0	0
Totals	39	10	15	10	3	7

Colorado	AB	R	H	RBI	BB	SO
Matsui, 2B	5	1	3	0	0	1
Tulowitzki, SS	4	1	1	0	1	1
Holliday, LF	5	1	1	3	0	0
Helton, 1B	4	1	1	0	1	1
Atkins, 3B	2	1	0	0	2	1
Hawpe, RF	5	0	2	1	0	2
Torrealba, C	5	0	2	1	0	0
Sullivan, CF	2	0	0	0	0	0
b-Spilborghs, PH-CF	2	0	0	0	0	0
Fogg, P	0	0	0	0	0	0
Morales, P	1	0	0	0	0	1
a-Smith, PH	1	0	1	0	0	0
Affeldt, P	0	0	0	0	0	0
c-Baker, PH	1	0	0	0	0	0
Herges, P	0	0	0	0	0	0
Fuentes, P	0	0	0	0	0	0
d-Taveras, PH	1	0	0	0	0	0
Hawkins, P	0	0	0	0	0	0
Totals	38	5	11	5	4	7

BATTING
2B: Lugo (1, Fogg), Ellsbury 3 (3, Fogg, Fogg, Fuentes), Ortiz (3, Fogg), Drew (2, Morales), Pedroia (1, Fuentes).
Team LOB: 7.

BASERUNNING
SB: Lowell (1, 3rd base off Hawkins/Torrealba).

FIELDING
E: Drew (1, missed catch).

PITCHING

Boston	IP	H	R	ER	BB	SO	HR
Matsuzaka (W, 1-0)	5.1	3	2	2	3	5	0
Lopez	0.0	2	0	0	0	0	0
Timlin (H, 1)	0.2	2	2	2	0	0	0
Okajima (H, 2)	1.0	2	1	1	0	2	1
Delcarmen	0.2	1	0	0	1	0	0
Papelbon (S, 2)	1.1	1	0	0	0	0	0

a-Singled for Morales in the 5th. b-Flied out for Sullivan in the 6th. c-Lined out for Affeldt in the 6th. d-Lined out for Fuentes in the 8th.

BATTING
3B: Hawpe (1, Papelbon).
HR: Holliday (1, 7th inning off Okajima, 2 on, 0 out).
Team LOB: 11.

BASERUNNING
SB: Matsui (1, 2nd base off Timlin/Varitek).

FIELDING
Outfield assists: Holliday (Ramirez at home).

PITCHING

Colorado	IP	H	R	ER	BB	SO	HR
Fogg (L, 0-1)	2.2	10	6	6	2	2	0
Morales	2.1	1	0	0	0	1	0
Affeldt	1.0	0	0	0	0	1	0
Herges	1.0	0	0	0	0	3	0
Fuentes	1.0	3	3	3	1	0	0
Hawkins	1.0	1	1	1	0	0	0

BOSTON 10, COLORADO 5

How sweep it is!

SOX SCALE PEAK AGAIN

By Jeff Horrigan
BOSTON HERALD
October 29, 2007

Back in 2004, New England cried collective tears of joy when the Red Sox brought 86 years of futility to a resounding end, exorcising the restless souls of lost generations that never had the opportunity to see their beloved team win a World Series title.

When the final out was made in St. Louis, fans dropped to their knees, offering prayers of thanks for a relatively effortless sweep in the Fall Classic after an unimaginable comeback in the American League Championship Series.

Three years later, everything is different. When the Sox defeated the Colorado Rockies, 4-3, at Coors Field last night to wrap up another four-game World Series sweep, many folks back home undoubtedly substituted satisfied smiles for tears, realizing that with the way the team is currently configured, championships could become regular occurrences, altering the way future generations view the franchise.

And this time, rather than dropping to their knees, Sox fans were more likely to leap off their sofa and join Jonathan Papelbon in a frantic Irish jig to celebrate the organization's seventh World Series triumph.

"When I came here in 2003, it seemed like it was impossible for this team to win a World Series, but this is my second now," David Ortiz said. "In life, when you work hard, things like this happen."

The Sox made short work of the Rockies, who came into the series on an unthinkable roll, having won 21 of 22 games to rise out of obscurity and storm to the National League pen-

Jonathan Papelbon leaps into the air following his strikeout of Seth Smith to end Game 4. *(Nancy Lane/Boston Herald)*

WORLD SERIES GAME 4

Mike Lowell sides into home to put the Sox up 2-0 on a Jason Varitek single in the fifth inning. *(Matthew West/Boston Herald)*

nant. The Sox outscored Colorado, 29-10, and out-performed the Rockies on the mound, at the plate and in the field.

It was only fitting that the storybook season had a fairy-tale ending. Jon Lester, who was undergoing chemotherapy to treat anaplastic large-cell lymphoma at this time last year, pitched 5 2/3 scoreless innings to become the first Sox lefty ever to earn the victory in a World Series-clinching game. The 23-year-old allowed only three hits, struck out three batters and held the Rockies hitless in five at-bats with runners in scoring position before making way for the bullpen.

"Words cannot describe how good this feels," Lester said in the champagne-soaked clubhouse. "It's been a whirlwind year for me. I don't know when it will sink in."

The Rockies mounted their only serious threat against Lester in the second inning, when Todd Helton lined a leadoff double and Brad Hawpe drew a two-out walk. Lester, however, extricated himself from the jam by getting Yorvit Torrealba to ground out.

The Sox jumped out to a 1-0 lead against Aaron Cook in the first inning when Jacoby Ellsbury, fresh off a four-hit performance on Saturday, lined a game-opening, opposite-field double down the left field line. He scored two batters later when Ortiz bounced a first-pitch fastball through the right side of the infield for a RBI single.

The Red Sox made it to 2-0 in the fifth, when Mike Lowell lined a leadoff double to the left-center field gap and scored two batters later on Jason Varitek's single just beyond the diving effort of the first baseman Helton.

Lowell, the series MVP, gave the Sox a 3-0 lead in the seventh when he drove Cook from the game

---

Jon Lester pitched 5 2/3 scoreless innings in Game 4. *(Matthew West/Boston Herald)*

BOSTON 4, COLORADO 3

WORLD SERIES GAME 4

by driving a knee-high sinker over the left field wall.

The Rockies finally broke through in the bottom of the seventh, when Hawpe crushed Manny Delcarmen's full-count fastball over the right field wall.

As was the case all season, the Sox immediately answered their opponents to halt any potential shift of momentum. This time, Bobby Kielty led off the eighth by slamming reliever Brian Fuentes' first

---

Bobby Kielty rounds the bases after hitting a pinch-hit home run in the eighth inning. *(John Wilcox/Boston Herald)*

pitch into the left-field seats for the 21st pinch-hit homer in World Series history and the first for a member of the Sox since Bernie Carbo's unforgettable, three-run shot on Oct. 21, 1975.

Kielty's clout proved vital because Garrett Atkins clubbed a two-run homer off Hideki Okajima in the eighth to narrow the lead to a single run before Papelbon came on to record the final five outs for his third save of the series.

"I knew I had to be ready for anything," Papelbon said. "I wanted to get as many key outs when they were needed. It's just amazing what's happened."

BOSTON 4, COLORADO 3 • OCTOBER 28, 2007

	1	2	3	4	5	6	7	8	9	R	H	E
Boston	1	0	0	0	1	0	1	1	0	4	9	0
Colorado	0	0	0	0	0	0	1	2	0	3	7	0

Boston	AB	R	H	RBI	BB	SO
Ellsbury, CF-LF	4	1	2	0	0	1
Pedroia, 2B	4	0	0	0	0	0
Ortiz, 1B	3	0	1	1	1	0
1-Crisp, PR-CF	0	0	0	0	0	0
Ramirez, LF	4	0	0	0	0	1
Okajima, P	0	0	0	0	0	0
Papelbon, P	0	0	0	0	0	0
Lowell, 3B	4	2	2	1	0	0
Drew, RF	4	0	0	0	0	1
Varitek, C	4	0	2	1	0	0
Lugo, SS	3	0	1	0	0	0
Lester, P	2	0	0	0	0	1
Delcarmen, P	0	0	0	0	0	0
Timlin, P	0	0	0	0	0	0
a-Kielty, PH	1	1	1	1	0	0
Youkilis, 1B	0	0	0	0	0	0
Totals	**33**	**4**	**9**	**4**	**1**	**4**

a-Homered for Timlin in the 8th.
1-Ran for Ortiz in the 8th.

BATTING
2B: Ellsbury (4, Cook), Lowell (3, Cook).
HR: Lowell (1, 7th inning off Cook, 0 on, 0 out), Kielty (1, 8th inning off Fuentes, 0 on, 0 out).
Team LOB: 3.

Boston	IP	H	R	ER	BB	SO	HR
Lester (W, 1-0)	5.2	3	0	0	3	3	0
Delcarmen (H, 1)	0.2	2	1	1	0	1	1
Timlin (H, 2)	0.2	0	0	0	0	2	0
Okajima (H, 3)	0.1	2	2	2	0	0	1
Papelbon (S, 3)	1.2	0	0	0	0	1	0

Colorado	AB	R	H	RBI	BB	SO
Matsui, 2B	4	0	1	0	0	1
Corpas, P	0	0	0	0	0	0
b-Smith, PH	1	0	0	0	0	1
Tulowitzki, SS	4	0	0	0	0	3
Holliday, LF	4	0	0	0	0	1
Helton, 1B	4	1	2	0	0	0
Atkins, 3B	3	1	1	2	1	0
Spilborghs, CF	3	0	0	0	1	1
Hawpe, RF	3	1	1	1	1	0
Torrealba, C	4	0	0	0	0	0
Cook, P	2	0	1	0	0	0
Affeldt, P	0	0	0	0	0	0
a-Sullivan, PH	1	0	1	0	0	0
Fuentes, P	0	0	0	0	0	0
Carroll, 2B	1	0	0	0	0	0
Totals	**34**	**3**	**7**	**3**	**3**	**7**

a-Singled for Affeldt in the 7th. b-Struck out for Corpas in the 9th.

BATTING
2B: Helton (2, Lester), Matsui (1, Lester).
HR: Hawpe (1, 7th inning off Delcarmen, 0 on, 0 out), Atkins (1, 8th inning off Okajima, 1 on, 1 out).
Team LOB: 7.

FIELDING
DP: 3 (Atkins-Matsui-Helton, Helton, Tulowitzki-Matsui-Helton).

Colorado	IP	H	R	ER	BB	SO	HR
Cook (L, 0-1)	6.0	6	3	3	0	2	1
Affeldt	1.0	1	0	0	0	1	0
Fuentes	0.2	2	1	1	1	0	1
Corpas	1.1	0	0	0	0	1	0

Simply the Most Valuable

By Rob Bradford
BOSTON HERALD
October 29, 2007

Maybe Mike Lowell should leave.

When you're standing on a baseball field clutching a World Series MVP trophy in the midst of being showered with deafening chants of "Re-sign Lowell!" from more than a thousand Red Sox fans, well, it can't really get much better.

"The coolest thing is that I'm instantly part of baseball history," Lowell said, deep in the postgame celebration. "It doesn't get better than that."

But the fact of the matter is, Lowell shouldn't leave. It was just that the big, bright neon sign defining the importance of the third baseman's presence just happened to be soaked with World Series wishes and champagne dreams.

"I don't want to imagine life without him," said Sox ace Josh Beckett, who came over from Florida with Lowell on that fateful Thanksgiving back in 2005. "I hope they re-sign him. But it's not up to me, it's up to him."

Hey, maybe, just maybe, this storybook ending to a fairy-tale season was what will put pen to paper and keep the third baseman collecting paychecks from Henry and not Hank or Hal (Steinbrenner, that is).

The reality is that if the fans of New England were doing the negotiating, all it would take is the picture of Lowell raising his arm, pointing to his family and pouncing on a celebratory pile he helped make happen and it would be a done deal.

"You can take that term 'throw-in' and throw it away," said Red Sox principal owner John Henry somewhere in the vicinity of a trophy-holding, cigar-smoking third baseman. "He's really deserving. It seems like we've been together throughout both our careers. I'm really happy for him."

Henry appreciates Lowell, as does Red Sox general manager Theo Epstein. It would be hard not to, simply going off the sight of the graying 33-year-old hitting .400 throughout the Red Sox' World Series sweep of the Rockies. And if there was a yearning for a slightly stronger punctuation, well, that came in the form of a crucial solo homer to lead off the seventh inning.

And the irony of the timing of the news that Alex Rodriguez was opting out of his contract with the Yankees and would be the "other" third baseman on the market as Lowell circled the bases only added to the future intrigue. (Along with chants of "Don't sign A-Rod" as the players drifted away from their Coors Field celebration.)

But bidding war, or not—free agency be darned—the fact was there was no more important teammate in the World Series championship clubhouse than Lowell.

"To be brutally honest, no," said Sox infielder Alex Cora, tearing up slightly as he talked about whether he could imagine life without Lowell. "It's not what he brings on the field, it's what he brings off the field. For me, Mikey is a better person than ballplayer."

WORLD SERIES MVP

Mike Lowell is congratulated by Julio Lugo after scoring in the fifth inning of Game 4. *(Stuart Cahill/Boston Herald)*

Judging by what Lowell did on the baseball diamond, that is a bold statement.

Will he ever have another year like the one he just completed in 2007? Maybe not. But there has to be something to the fact that even the fans who never have gotten a peek behind the Red Sox' clubhouse curtain understand there is more to the man than projections and promise.

Sure, other leaders and legends have come and gone from the Red Sox and they seemed to land on their feet. But Lowell is a different sort of glue than the likes of Kevin Millar presented.

No player under the current regime has supplied the presence of Lowell. Not one. If there is any

doubt, go to the four corners of the Red Sox clubhouse and ask.

"The whole business side is going to take place," said Red Sox outfielder J.D. Drew. "He's as much a part of this team as anybody I ever played with."

"He's simply," said Sox infielder Eric Hinske, "the man."

It is a fact that is hard to argue. Hopefully John Henry won't.

Festive release

CHAMPS LET LOOSE WITH WILD, EMOTIONAL PARTY

By Michael Silverman
BOSTON HERALD
October 29, 2007

Champagne and beer droplets hung from the white and silver ceiling of the visitors' clubhouse at Coors Field after the Red Sox won the World Series last night.

It looked like an ice palace, but the steam and heat from an emotional championship team melted the scene as the celebration commenced.

After Jonathan Papelbon whipped off his hat and threw his glove over his head upon striking out Seth Smith to end the game, the Red Sox whooped it up.

After a massive group hug near the mound started by catcher Jason Varitek jumping into Papelbon's arms, the party moved to the clubhouse.

Massage therapist Russell Nua donned his blue goggles and joined the fray. David Ortiz, delayed by some interview or another, finally broke free with a "Hey, (expletives), wait for me!"

A table in the middle of the clubhouse served as a holding tray for the tubs of ice, champagne and beer, and also as a temporary rostrum for anyone who wanted to get up and speak — holding the trophy, of course.

Ortiz bounced and danced and jiggled in place as he was sprayed from 20 directions with bubbly. At one point he pointed to his World Series champions T-shirt and yelled, "When you wear 'Red Sox' on your shirt, you're good at something, (expletives)."

Josh Beckett looked at the trophy and yelled, "This is what all the hard work is for," and then got utterly doused by a well-

Jacoby Ellsbury douses Bobby Kielty with champagne following the Red Sox' sweep of the Rockies in the World Series. *(Matthew West/Boston Herald)*

WORLD SERIES GAME 4

BOSTON 4, COLORADO 3

aimed bottle of Domaine Ste. Michelle Brut. "I'm going to hand this off so I don't get sprayed anymore."

Papelbon had his turn: "This goes to the baddest team in the (expletive) big leagues."

Royce Clayton, who had a total of six at-bats for the Sox in the regular season and was left off the playoff roster, was called up to the table. In the majors since 1991 without a World Series appearance, Clayton cried into the shoulder of Ortiz, then spoke.

"I love you guys, I love all of you," the 37-year-old said before catching his breath. "I waited all these years and all I can say is, 'Woo-woo, woo-woo!'"

The party was back on.

Assistant trainer Masai Takahashi shook up cans of beer, opened them and poured them down the back of revelers' T-shirts.

Daisuke Matsuzaka looked in awe at the World Series trophy and held court with the Japanese media with a smile on his face. He and his interpreter, Masa Hoshino, shared a heartfelt hug in the middle of the clubhouse.

Bryan Corey walked around the room silently videotaping the proceedings.

Kevin Youkilis roared to head trainer Paul Lessard, "You bald SOB!" before their bear hug.

Advance scout Todd Claus complained, without really complaining and to nobody in particular, "I just got a beer poured in my ear."

The longest-tenured member of the team, Tim Wakefield (who was left off the World Series roster because of a bad shoulder), could not stop grinning.

Dustin Pedroia lets loose a spray of champagne. *(Matthew West/Boston Herald)*

WORLD SERIES GAME 4

BOSTON 4, COLORADO 3

WORLD SERIES GAME 4

Coco Crisp and Jacoby Ellsbury celebrate the second Red Sox World Series title in four years. *(Matthew West/Boston Herald)*

"I'm happy and very blessed to say I'm a two-time champion," he said. "We're ready for the parade."

John Henry, principal owner of the team, kept using reporters as human shields to ward off liquid attacks.

Back on the field after the champagne bath, Mike Timlin bowed to the crowd.

David Ortiz and Jonathan Papelbon clown around with the World Series trophy. *(Matthew West/Boston Herald)*

The Sox fans hanging around in the stands started a couple of chants. One was "Don't sign A-Rod." The other, "Re-sign Lowell."

Varitek held back tears but could not keep a deep current of emotion from showing in his voice as he spoke of the battle that the winning pitcher, Jon Lester, displayed — not just in the game, but in his battle back from cancer.

"We're talking about life, not a game," said Varitek.

Last night, the Red Sox celebrated both.

2007 REGULAR SEASON STATISTICS

Batting

Player	G	AB	R	H	2B	3B	HR	RBI	TB	BB	SO	SB	CS	OBP	SLG	AVG
M Lowell	154	589	79	191	37	2	21	120	295	53	71	3	2	.378	.501	.324
J Lugo	147	570	71	135	36	2	8	73	199	48	82	33	6	.294	.349	.237
D Ortiz	149	549	116	182	52	1	35	117	341	111	103	3	1	.445	.621	.332
K Youkilis	145	528	85	152	35	2	16	83	239	77	105	4	2	.390	.453	.288
C Crisp	145	526	85	141	28	7	6	60	201	50	84	28	6	.330	.382	.268
D Pedroia	139	520	86	165	39	1	8	50	230	47	42	7	1	.380	.442	.317
M Ramirez	133	483	84	143	33	1	20	88	238	71	92	0	0	.388	.493	.296
J Drew	140	466	84	126	30	4	11	64	197	79	100	4	2	.373	.423	.270
J Varitek	131	435	57	111	15	3	17	68	183	71	122	1	2	.367	.421	.255
A Cora	83	207	30	51	10	5	3	18	80	7	23	1	1	.298	.386	.246
R Clayton	77	195	24	48	14	0	1	12	65	14	53	2	1	.296	.333	.246
E Hinske	84	186	25	38	12	3	6	21	74	28	54	3	0	.317	.398	.204
W Pena	73	156	18	34	9	1	5	17	60	14	58	0	1	.291	.385	.218
J Ellsbury	33	116	20	41	7	1	3	18	59	8	15	9	0	.394	.509	.353
D Mirabelli	48	114	9	23	3	0	5	16	41	11	41	0	0	.278	.360	.202
B Kielty	33	87	10	19	3	0	1	12	25	8	26	0	0	.287	.287	.218
K Cash	12	27	2	3	1	0	0	4	4	4	13	0	0	.242	.148	.111
B Moss	15	25	6	7	2	1	0	1	11	4	6	0	0	.379	.440	.280
J Beckett	3	11	1	2	1	0	0	1	3	0	1	0	0	.182	.273	.182
J Bailey	3	9	1	1	0	0	1	1	4	0	1	0	0	.111	.444	.111
D Matsuzaka	2	4	0	0	0	0	0	0	0	0	2	0	0	.000	.000	.000
J Tavarez	2	4	0	1	0	0	0	0	1	1	3	0	0	.400	.250	.250
C Schilling	1	2	0	1	0	0	0	0	1	0	1	0	0	.500	.500	.500
T Wakefield	1	2	0	0	0	0	0	0	0	0	2	0	0	.000	.000	.000
M Delcarmen	2	0	0	0	0	0	0	0	0	0	0	0	0	.000	.000	.000
B Donnelly	2	0	0	0	0	0	0	0	0	0	0	0	0	.000	.000	.000
J Lopez	3	0	0	0	0	0	0	0	0	0	0	0	0	.000	.000	.000
H Okajima	3	0	0	0	0	0	0	0	0	0	0	0	0	.000	.000	.000
J Papelbon	4	0	0	0	0	0	0	0	0	0	0	0	0	.000	.000	.000
J Pineiro	2	0	0	0	0	0	0	0	0	0	0	0	0	.000	.000	.000
K Snyder	3	0	0	0	0	0	0	0	0	0	0	0	0	.000	.000	.000
M Timlin	4	0	0	0	0	0	0	0	0	0	0	0	0	.000	.000	.000

Pitching

Player	W	L	ERA	G	SV	SVO	IP	H	R	ER	BB	SO
D Matsuzaka	15	12	4.40	32	0	0	204.2	191	25	13	80	201
J Beckett	20	7	3.27	30	0	0	200.2	189	76	73	40	194
T Wakefield	17	12	4.76	31	0	0	189.0	191	104	100	64	110
C Schilling	9	8	3.87	240	0	1	151.0	165	68	65	23	101
J Tavarez	7	11	5.15	340	0	0	134.2	151	89	77	51	77
H Okajima	3	2	2.22	665	7	0	69.0	50	17	17	17	63
J Lester	4	0	4.57	12	0	0	63.0	61	33	32	31	50
J Papelbon	1	3	1.85	59	37	40	58.1	30	12	12	15	84
M Timlin	2	1	3.42	50	1	1	55.1	46	23	21	7	31
K Snyder	2	3	3.81	46	0	0	54.1	45	29	23	32	41
E Gagne	4	2	3.81	54	16	20	52.0	49	22	22	21	51
M Delcarmen	0	0	2.05	44	1	2	44.0	28	11	10	17	41
J Lopez	2	1	3.10	61	0	2	40.2	36	16	14	18	26
J Pineiro	1	1	5.03	31	0	0	34.0	41	20	19	14	20
C Buchholz	3	1	1.59	4	0	0	22.2	14	6	4	10	22
B Donnelly	2	1	3.05	27	0	0	20.2	19	8	7	5	15
J Romero	1	0	3.15	23	1	1	20.0	24	7	7	15	11
B Corey	1	0	1.93	9	0	0	9.1	6	2	2	4	6
D Hansack	0	1	4.70	3	0	0	7.2	9	5	4	5	5